4

Sequenti
Spelling

Student Workbook

serve
reserve
preserve
conserve
deserve
service

Day 1

Spelling Lesson:

As you hear them, write the spelling words for the day in the space provided. Be sure that you correct any words you have spelled incorrectly.

1. _____
2. _____
3. _____
4. _____
5. _____
6. _____
7. _____
8. _____
9. _____
10. _____
11. _____
12. _____
13. _____

14. _____
15. _____
16. _____
17. _____
18. _____
19. _____
20. _____
21. _____
22. _____
23. _____
24. _____
25. _____

Using Your Words:

Fill in the blanks with words from today's spelling list.

1. In some denominations, there is a _____ council.

2. It was _____ of you to think your dad wouldn't notice the dent in the car.

3. How much work do you have to _____? I want to go to the mall.

4. What did you _____ today?

5. My friend Paula is half _____. Her father immigrated last year.

6. Did anyone _____ in the fire last year?

7. Don't you think you're being a little _____?

8. My mom teaches _____ at the high school.

9. Alicia's feet are very _____.

10. Jon broke his ankle in two places in a very _____ bike accident.

Day 2

Spelling Lesson:

As you hear them, write the spelling words for the day in the space provided. Be sure that you correct any words you have spelled incorrectly.

1. _____

2. _____

3. _____

4. _____

5. _____

6. _____

7. _____

8. _____

9. _____

10. _____

11. _____

12. _____

13. _____

14. _____

15. _____

16. _____

17. _____

18. _____

19. _____

20. _____

21. _____

22. _____

23. _____

24. _____

25. _____

Using Your Words:

Adjectives

Many of today's words are adjectives. Adjectives are words which are used to modify nouns or pronouns. Use three of them in a sentence correctly.

_____

_____

_____

_____

_____

_____

_____

_____

Day 3

Spelling Lesson:

As you hear them, write the spelling words for the day in the space provided. Be sure that you correct any words you have spelled incorrectly.

1. _____

2. _____

3. _____

4. _____

5. _____

6. _____

7. _____

8. _____

9. _____

10. _____

11. _____

12. _____

13. _____

14. _____

15. _____

16. _____

17. _____

18. _____

19. _____

20. _____

21. _____

22. _____

23. _____

24. _____

25. _____

Using Your Words:

Unscramble these:

1. eprehlisab _____

2. nihsdelutnossa _____

3. lseispoh _____

4. hrlsi _____

5. wehiJs _____

6. vledtriy _____

7. esolsdr _____

8. getuon _____

9. epdioccmhals _____

10. elsehidr _____

Spelling Lesson:

As you hear them, write the spelling words for the day in the space provided. Be sure that you correct any words you have spelled incorrectly.

1. _____

2. _____

3. _____

4. _____

5. _____

6. _____

7. _____

8. _____

9. _____

10. _____

11. _____

12. _____

13. _____

14. _____

15. _____

16. _____

17. _____

18. _____

19. _____

20. _____

21. _____

22. _____

23. _____

24. _____

25. _____

Using Your Words:

\

Can you  the words?

S D T Y H X V T H A Q G G S Y
K T T I W S Q Q H S N A P Z H
C O N S Y Q O A J I I A B S J
X R I E Z R Q L H X N N I C E
Z S D P M E S S D I R N N P Z
D Y E H N H I X S E A Q I I K
S N H L I L S H L D R T X R F
E N S I O V Q I X S H E W U N
U D I P P L T U L P R K D B A
G Q N V M H K R O P O Q H B F
N M I M C X H P H X M S E I I
O R F S T U D E N T S O C S K
T V N D A T H E I R Y P C H T
U D U Y H N U I G L V D I C C
U U B F U Z A H S I T I R B A

Words Used

accomplishments

British

Danish

Finnish

polishing

rubbish

soldered

Spanish

students

their

tongues

unfinished

Day 5

As you hear them, write the spelling words for the day in the space provided. Be sure that you correct any words you have spelled incorrectly.

1. _____

2. _____

3. _____

4. _____

5. _____

6. _____

7. _____

8. _____

9. _____

10. _____

11. _____

12. _____

13. _____

14. _____

15. _____

16. _____

17. _____

18. _____

19. _____

20. _____

21. _____

22. _____

23. _____

24. _____

25. _____

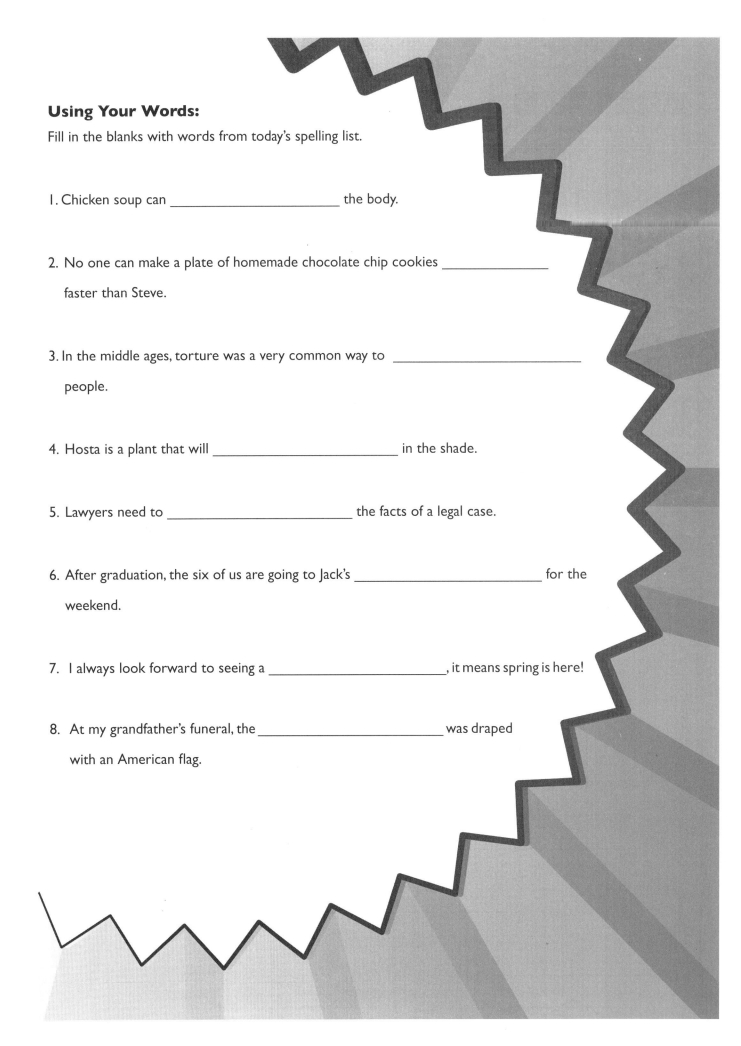

Using Your Words:

Fill in the blanks with words from today's spelling list.

1. Chicken soup can _____ the body.

2. No one can make a plate of homemade chocolate chip cookies _____

   faster than Steve.

3. In the middle ages, torture was a very common way to _____

   people.

4. Hosta is a plant that will _____ in the shade.

5. Lawyers need to _____ the facts of a legal case.

6. After graduation, the six of us are going to Jack's _____ for the

   weekend.

7. I always look forward to seeing a _____, it means spring is here!

8. At my grandfather's funeral, the _____ was draped

   with an American flag.

Day 6

Spelling Lesson:

As you hear them, write the spelling words for the day in the space provided. Be sure that you correct any words you have spelled incorrectly.

1. _____

2. _____

3. _____

4. _____

5. _____

6. _____

7. _____

8. _____

9. _____

10. _____

11. _____

12. _____

13. _____

14. _____

15. _____

16. _____

17. _____

18. _____

19. _____

20. _____

21. _____

22. _____

23. _____

24. _____

25. _____

Using Your Words:

Choose seven of the words from today's list and use each in a sentence.

1. _____

2. _____

3. _____

4. _____

5. _____

6. _____

7. _____

Day 7

Spelling Lesson:

As you hear them, write the spelling words for the day in the space provided. Be sure that you correct any words you have spelled incorrectly.

1. _____

2. _____

3. _____

4. _____

5. _____

6. _____

7. _____

8. _____

9. _____

10. _____

11. _____

12. _____

13. _____

14. _____

15. _____

16. _____

17. _____

18. _____

19. _____

20. _____

21. _____

22. _____

23. _____

24. _____

25. _____

Using Your Words:

Unscramble these:

1. erdimkhsis _____

2. hpnudsie _____

3. sgohunrnii _____

4. baetsedshil _____

5. hienddsmii _____

6. hotisnsade _____

7. fiafparn _____

8. gnfamuarif _____

9. bicenat _____

10. lsdemiblehe _____

Day 8

Spelling Lesson:

As you hear them, write the spelling words for the day in the space provided. Be sure that you correct any words you have spelled incorrectly.

1. _____

2. _____

3. _____

4. _____

5. _____

6. _____

7. _____

8. _____

9. _____

10. _____

11. _____

12. _____

13. _____

14. _____

15. _____

16. _____

17. _____

18. _____

19. _____

20. _____

21. _____

22. _____

23. _____

24. _____

25. _____

Using Your Words:
Choose seven of the words from your spelling list and use each of them in a sentence. Or write a short pagraph or silly story using all of them.

1. _____

_____

2. _____

_____

3. _____

_____

4. _____

_____

5. _____

_____

6. _____

_____

7. _____

_____

Sequential Spelling Level 4 - Student Workbook

Day 9

As you hear them, write the spelling words for the day in the space provided. Be sure that you correct any words you have spelled incorrectly.

1._____

2._____

3._____

4._____

5._____

6._____

7._____

8._____

9._____

10. _____

11. _____

12. _____

13. _____

14. _____

15. _____

16. _____

17. _____

18. _____

19._____

20. _____

21. _____

22. _____

23. _____

24. _____

25. _____

Using Your Words:

Funny spellings and sounds

Use each of these words
correctly in a sentence.

Soldier	**"SOH'l jur"**
solder	**"SAH dur"**
solid	**"SAH' lid"**
solider	**"SAH' lid ur"**
tongue	**"Tung"**

1._____

_____

2._____

_____

3._____

_____

4._____

_____

5._____

_____

Spelling Lesson:

As you hear them, write the spelling words for the day in the space provided. Be sure that you correct any words you have spelled incorrectly.

1. _____

2. _____

3. _____

4. _____

5. _____

6. _____

7. _____

8. _____

9. _____

10. _____

11. _____

12. _____

13. _____

14. _____

15. _____

16. _____

17. _____

18. _____

19. _____

20. _____

21. _____

22. _____

23. _____

24. _____

25. _____

Using Your Words:

Make as many words as you can from the letters in word.

assassinates

_____

_____

_____

_____

_____

_____

_____

_____

_____

_____

Day 11

Spelling Lesson:

As you hear them, write the spelling words for the day in the space provided. Be sure that you correct any words you have spelled incorrectly.

1. _____

2. _____

3. _____

4. _____

5. _____

6. _____

7. _____

8. _____

9. _____

10. _____

11. _____

12. _____

13. _____

14. _____

15. _____

16. _____

17. _____

18. _____

19. _____

20. _____

21. _____

22. _____

23. _____

24. _____

25. _____

Using Your Words:

Sound alike words:

Fill in the blanks with words from your spelling list.

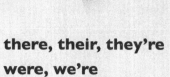

there, their, they're
were, we're
your, you're

1. Nathan ate dinner at _____ house.

2. Paul, _____ friend left a message for you.

3. _____ on our way to the movies.

4. Carter said _____ coming over tonight.

5. Because of the rain, there _____ delays at the airport.

6. I think_____ the best friend ever!

7. _____ is an exciting movie playing at the theatre this weekend.

8. Did you finish _____ chores yet?

9. You can have another cookie if _____ is one left.

10. _____ always late!

Spelling Lesson:

As you hear them, write the spelling words for the day in the space provided. Be sure that you correct any words you have spelled incorrectly.

1. _____

2. _____

3. _____

4. _____

5. _____

6. _____

7. _____

8. _____

9. _____

10. _____

11. _____

12. _____

13. _____

14. _____

15. _____

16. _____

17. _____

18. _____

19. _____

20. _____

21. _____

22. _____

23. _____

24. _____

25. _____

Using Your Words:

Can you find the words?

```
X  N  T  O  X  I  N  S  P  Y  N  X  Y  A  Y
H  X  O  H  O  E  X  E  Y  I  Q  L  S  A  L
I  A  B  I  M  C  N  O  L  K  D  S  S  Q  L
J  Z  I  X  T  G  C  L  I  I  A  H  E  N  A
W  O  F  R  U  A  I  F  L  S  S  H  U  G  N
L  F  M  I  P  C  C  O  S  Y  Q  X  G  X  I
I  Z  N  Z  I  I  S  I  R  H  O  X  N  S  G
X  S  T  N  U  N  N  T  X  T  S  E  O  O  R
L  R  E  D  N  A  Y  S  C  O  N  X  T  L  A
M  P  M  I  T  R  R  N  R  K  T  N  K  D  M
D  E  A  I  S  O  L  D  E  R  I  N  G  I  L
S  T  O  D  E  S  O  P  P  U  S  V  I  E  A
G  N  I  T  A  N  I  S  S  A  S  S  A  R  I
S  D  E  S  H  E  C  R  G  A  Y  I  T  S  Y
E  F  L  I  X  P  O  J  Z  B  H  X  C  P  M
```

Words used

assassinating

assassinations

hairpins

intoxication

marginally

penguins

penicillin

soldering

soldiers

solidly

supposed

tongues

toxins

Day 13

Spelling Lesson:

As you hear them, write the spelling words for the day in the space provided. Be sure that you correct any words you have spelled incorrectly.

1. _____

2. _____

3. _____

4. _____

5. _____

6. _____

7. _____

8. _____

9. _____

10. _____

11. _____

12. _____

13. _____

14. _____

15. _____

16. _____

17. _____

18. _____

19. _____

20. _____

21. _____

22. _____

23. _____

24. _____

25. _____

Using Your Words:

Use a dictionary to find the definitions of these words; then use each of them in a sentence.

1. brigand _____

_____

2. stipend _____

_____

3. gantry _____

_____

4. sultry _____

_____

5. starling _____

_____

6. midland _____

_____

Day 14

Spelling Lesson:

As you hear them, write the spelling words for the day in the space provided. Be sure that you correct any words you have spelled incorrectly.

1. _____

2. _____

3. _____

4. _____

5. _____

6. _____

7. _____

8. _____

9. _____

10. _____

11. _____

12. _____

13. _____

14. _____

15. _____

16. _____

17. _____

18. _____

19. _____

20. _____

21. _____

22. _____

23. _____

24. _____

25. _____

Using Your Words:

Sound alike words:

Choose the correct word
for each sentence.

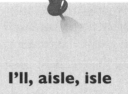

I'll, aisle, isle

1. _____be coming to your party.

2. The book is on the floor in the _____.

3. This _____ is a dream come true.

4. She looked beautiful walking down the _____ at the wedding.

5. _____ make the dip if you buy the chips.

6. Mark said the _____was deserted.

7. _____ 7 needs to be cleaned.

8. It was a tropical _____.

9. It's such a pretty _____ with flowers on the benches.

10. _____ walk you to your car.

Day 15

Spelling Lesson:

As you hear them, write the spelling words for the day in the space provided. Be sure that you correct any words you have spelled incorrectly.

1. _____

2. _____

3. _____

4. _____

5. _____

6. _____

7. _____

8. _____

9. _____

10. _____

11. _____

12. _____

13. _____

14. _____

15. _____

16. _____

17. _____

18. _____

19. _____

20. _____

21. _____

22. _____

23. _____

24. _____

25. _____

Using Your Words:

Unscramble these:

1. iglfgledn _____

2. inalds _____

3. esil _____

4. iseal _____

5. noihngt _____

6. ndkicgiu _____

7. itwrne _____

8. ntiryw _____

9. raprnetyc _____

10. erptstay _____

Day 16

As you hear them, write the spelling words for the day in the space provided. Be sure that you correct any words you have spelled incorrectly.

1. _____

2. _____

3. _____

4. _____

5. _____

6. _____

7. _____

8. _____

9. _____

10. _____

11. _____

12. _____

13. _____

14. _____

15. _____

16. _____

17. _____

18. _____

19. _____

20. _____

21. _____

22. _____

23. _____

24. _____

25. _____

Using Your Words:

Choose seven of the words from your spelling list and use each of them in a sentence. Or write a short paragraph or silly story using all of them.

1. _____

_____

2. _____

_____

3. _____

_____

4. _____

_____

5. _____

_____

6. _____

_____

7. _____

_____

Day 17

Spelling Lesson:

As you hear them, write the spelling words for the day in the space provided. Be sure that you correct any words you have spelled incorrectly.

1. _____

2. _____

3. _____

4. _____

5. _____

6. _____

7. _____

8. _____

9. _____

10. _____

11. _____

12. _____

13. _____

14. _____

15. _____

16. _____

17. _____

18. _____

19. _____

20. _____

21. _____

22. _____

23. _____

24. _____

25. _____

Using Your Words:

Sound alike words:

Use a dictionary to find the meanings of the words you don't know. Then, use each of them correctly in a sentence.

pedlar/peddler
cellar/seller
liar/lyre
friar/fryer/frier

1. pedlar _____

_____

2. peddler _____

_____

3. cellar _____

_____

4. seller _____

_____

5. liar _____

_____

6. lyre _____

_____

7. friar _____

_____

8. frier _____

_____

9. fryer _____

_____

Day 18

Spelling Lesson:

As you hear them, write the spelling words for the day in the space provided. Be sure that you correct any words you have spelled incorrectly.

1. _____

2. _____

3. _____

4. _____

5. _____

6. _____

7. _____

8. _____

9. _____

10. _____

11. _____

12. _____

13. _____

14. _____

15. _____

16. _____

17. _____

18. _____

19. _____

20. _____

21. _____

22. _____

23. _____

24. _____

25. _____

Using Your Words:

List as many words as you can that have the following letters (in order) in them:

lar

iar

_____

_____

_____

_____

_____

_____

_____

_____

_____

_____

Day 19

Spelling Lesson:

As you hear them, write the spelling words for the day in the space provided. Be sure that you correct any words you have spelled incorrectly.

1. _____

2. _____

3. _____

4. _____

5. _____

6. _____

7. _____

8. _____

9. _____

10. _____

11. _____

12. _____

13. _____

14. _____

15. _____

16. _____

17. _____

18. _____

19. _____

20. _____

21. _____

22. _____

23. _____

24. _____

25. _____

Using Your Words:

Fill in the blanks with the words from your spelling list.

1. The cliffs were almost _____ to the sea.

2. Who is the most _____ entertainer of your generation?

3. What a _____ looking hat!

4. This _____ sound went on and on.

5. The audience stood and _____ loudly when she finished her solo.

6. What a _____ sunset!

7. She's a _____ customer.

8. Even though Jack is very fit and _____, he hurt his back while

   digging in the yard.

Spelling Lesson:

As you hear them, write the spelling words for the day in the space provided. Be sure that you correct any words you have spelled incorrectly.

1. _____

2. _____

3. _____

4. _____

5. _____

6. _____

7. _____

8. _____

9. _____

10. _____

11. _____

12. _____

13. _____

14. _____

15. _____

16. _____

17. _____

18. _____

19. _____

20. _____

21. _____

22. _____

23. _____

24. _____

25. _____

Using Your Words:

\

Can you  the words?

```
R  L  M  F  Y  R  N  B  D  Y  A  C  S  S  O
W  D  X  U  G  T  B  A  T  G  I  P  P  O  F
Y  J  H  Q  S  R  I  I  G  R  S  H  I  L  L
I  L  V  F  V  C  R  R  C  Q  J  H  H  D  Z
J  B  R  Z  M  A  L  U  A  B  E  X  S  E  B
D  E  K  A  L  A  L  E  V  L  Z  H  R  R  G
R  E  G  U  L  A  R  I  T  Y  O  E  A  I  N
G  A  P  M  R  U  F  A  Y  Q  F  P  L  N  Z
S  O  K  O  V  M  C  J  U  I  T  S  O  G  Y
P  R  G  L  N  K  I  I  R  D  E  P  H  N  I
E  S  U  A  L  P  P  A  T  L  I  H  C  I  T
O  U  B  R  L  U  O  S  B  R  U  N  S  B  D
U  K  P  D  S  C  K  U  H  Q  A  K  G  U  O
R  E  Z  P  S  W  A  S  Y  G  Y  P  T  A  R
Z  D  C  V  Y  B  C  I  R  C  L  E  G  D  E
```

Words used

applause

baubles

circle

circular

daubing

marauding

molar

muscle

particularly

polarity

popularity

regularity

scholarships

soldering

Spelling Lesson:

As you hear them, write the spelling words for the day in the space provided. Be sure that you correct any words you have spelled incorrectly.

1. _____

2. _____

3. _____

4. _____

5. _____

6. _____

7. _____

8. _____

9. _____

10. _____

11. _____

12. _____

13. _____

14. _____

15. _____

16. _____

17. _____

18. _____

19. _____

20. _____

21. _____

22. _____

23. _____

24. _____

25. _____

Using Your Words:

Sound alike words:

Circle the appropriate word
to complete each sentence.

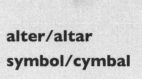

alter/altar

symbol/cymbal

1. Please kneel at the (alter, altar).

2. A distaff os a (cymbal, symbol) of the home.

3. We will need to (alter, altar) our travel arrangements.

4. My little brother cries when he hears a (cymbal, symbol) crash.

5. The robber tried to (alter, altar) his appearance.

6. A heart is the (cymbal, symbol) for love.

7. The bride and groom held hands as they approached the (alter, altar)

8. Can you play a finger (cymbal, symbol)?

Spelling Lesson:

As you hear them, write the spelling words for the day in the space provided. Be sure that you correct any words you have spelled incorrectly.

1. _____

2. _____

3. _____

4. _____

5. _____

6. _____

7. _____

8. _____

9. _____

10. _____

11. _____

12. _____

13. _____

14. _____

15. _____

16. _____

17. _____

18. _____

19. _____

20. _____

21. _____

22. _____

23. _____

24. _____

25. _____

Using Your Words:

Unscramble these:

1. enmceiid _____

2. sngiel _____

3. raugnsli _____

4. gneal _____

5. agnlaru _____

6. heodmt _____

7. cfrfiat _____

8. opsdire _____

9. ciamg _____

10. eiretlcc _____

Spelling Lesson:

As you hear them, write the spelling words for the day in the space provided. Be sure that you correct any words you have spelled incorrectly.

1. _____

2. _____

3. _____

4. _____

5. _____

6. _____

7. _____

8. _____

9. _____

10. _____

11. _____

12. _____

13. _____

14. _____

15. _____

16. _____

17. _____

18. _____

19. _____

20. _____

21. _____

22. _____

23. _____

24. _____

25. _____

Using Your Words:

Choose seven of the words in your spelling list and use each word in a sentence.

1._____

_____

2._____

_____

3._____

_____

4._____

_____

5._____

_____

6._____

_____

7._____

_____

Spelling Lesson:

As you hear them, write the spelling words for the day in the space provided. Be sure that you correct any words you have spelled incorrectly.

1. _____

2. _____

3. _____

4. _____

5. _____

6. _____

7. _____

8. _____

9. _____

10. _____

11. _____

12. _____

13. _____

14. _____

15. _____

16. _____

17. _____

18. _____

19. _____

20. _____

21. _____

22. _____

23. _____

24. _____

25. _____

Using Your Words:

List as many words as you can that have the following letters (in order) in them.

ian
lar

Spelling Lesson:

As you hear them, write the spelling words for the day in the space provided. Be sure that you correct any words you have spelled incorrectly.

1. _____

2. _____

3. _____

4. _____

5. _____

6. _____

7. _____

8. _____

9. _____

10. _____

11. _____

12. _____

13. _____

14. _____

15. _____

16. _____

17. _____

18. _____

19. _____

20. _____

21. _____

22. _____

23. _____

24. _____

25. _____

Using Your Words:

Fill in the blanks with words from today's spelling list:.

1. In the summer, we like to take a _____ lunch

    to the beach.

2. Lisa called me in a _____ because she couldn't

    find her car keys.

3. Jack attempted to _____ Steve's football moves with

    little success

4. I spent most of the afternoon at the _____ waiting to see the doctor.

5. Jon's _____ told him that the used car would need

    lots of repairs so he decided not to buy it.

6. We're going to spend our summer vacation near the _____ this year.

7. The paramedics arrived on the _____ minutes after the car crash.

8. Ulysses was a _____ of the Trojan Wars.

9. My mom bought me some beautiful batik _____ while she was in Bali.

10. Before going camping, we stocked up on the _____ necessities,

    peanut butter and jelly.

Spelling Lesson:

As you hear them, write the spelling words for the day in the space provided. Be sure that you correct any words you have spelled incorrectly.

1. _____

2. _____

3. _____

4. _____

5. _____

6. _____

7. _____

8. _____

9. _____

10. _____

11. _____

12. _____

13. _____

14. _____

15. _____

16. _____

17. _____

18. _____

19. _____

20. _____

21. _____

22. _____

23. _____

24. _____

25. _____

Using Your Words:

Choose seven words from your spelling list and use each of them in a sentence.

1. _____

_____

2. _____

_____

3. _____

_____

4. _____

_____

5. _____

_____

6. _____

_____

7. _____

_____

Spelling Lesson:

As you hear them, write the spelling words for the day in the space provided. Be sure that you correct any words you have spelled incorrectly.

1. _____

2. _____

3. _____

4. _____

5. _____

6. _____

7. _____

8. _____

9. _____

10. _____

11. _____

12. _____

13. _____

14. _____

15. _____

16. _____

17. _____

18. _____

19. _____

20. _____

21. _____

22. _____

23. _____

24. _____

25. _____

Using Your Words:

Unscramble these:

1. eidpcicnk _____

2. sphcsyi _____

3. ibsettscro _____

4. ceakdpni _____

5. myceocloinal _____

6. mcdkeimi _____

7. ardma _____

8. ftnacia _____

9. laafctani _____

10. tricdmaa _____

Sequential Spelling Level 4 - Student Workbook

As you hear them, write the spelling words for the day in the space provided. Be sure that you correct any words you have spelled incorrectly.

1. _____

2. _____

3. _____

4. _____

5. _____

6. _____

7. _____

8. _____

9. _____

10. _____

11. _____

12. _____

13. _____

14. _____

15. _____

16. _____

17. _____

18. _____

19. _____

20. _____

21. _____

22. _____

23. _____

24. _____

25. _____

Using Your Words:

\

Can you  the words?

```
Y  P  Y  L  E  K  Y  M  R  X  Y  G  D  E  M
P  L  I  L  A  Z  U  Z  E  L  I  N  I  Z  Z
Z  A  L  C  L  C  Q  R  L  W  X  I  P  I  P
N  P  N  A  N  A  I  A  T  R  K  Z  L  G  H
N  I  U  I  C  I  C  R  L  K  B  I  O  O  Y
A  Z  L  D  C  I  C  I  Y  I  O  M  M  L  S
L  I  I  A  T  K  T  K  M  L  B  O  A  O  I
T  P  B  A  N  U  I  A  I  O  P  N  T  P  C
Y  K  N  Q  P  J  Y  N  M  N  C  O  I  A  I
U  A  A  S  H  V  W  N  G  A  G  C  C  F  A
F  S  E  T  E  B  A  I  D  O  R  E  O  C  N
F  R  A  N  T  I  C  A  L  L  Y  D  X  I  W
A  C  I  T  C  R  A  T  N  A  Q  H  P  G  G
F  R  L  N  H  B  Y  F  O  L  L  D  W  M  R
M  B  Q  F  C  M  I  M  I  C  K  I  N  G  T
```

Words Used

antarctica

apologize

comically

diabetes

diplomatic

dramatically

economizing

fanatically

frantically

lyrical

mimicking

panicking

psysician

picnicking

Spelling Lesson:

As you hear them, write the spelling words for the day in the space provided. Be sure that you correct any words you have spelled incorrectly.

1. _____

2. _____

3. _____

4. _____

5. _____

6. _____

7. _____

8. _____

9. _____

10. _____

11. _____

12. _____

13. _____

14. _____

15. _____

16. _____

17. _____

18. _____

19. _____

20. _____

21. _____

22. _____

23. _____

24. _____

25. _____

Using Your Words:

:

List as many words as you can with the following letters (in order) in them.

ace

ice

_____

_____

_____

_____

_____

_____

_____

_____

_____

Spelling Lesson:

As you hear them, write the spelling words for the day in the space provided. Be sure that you correct any words you have spelled incorrectly.

1. _____

2. _____

3. _____

4. _____

5. _____

6. _____

7. _____

8. _____

9. _____

10. _____

11. _____

12. _____

13. _____

14. _____

15. _____

16. _____

17. _____

18. _____

19. _____

20. _____

21. _____

22. _____

23. _____

24. _____

25. _____

Using Your Words:

Unscramble these:

1. pcaeulpe _____

2. arkmepaece _____

3. suearscf _____

4. srecvise _____

5. meiopssr _____

6. nceteipaeps _____

7. eidpsurejc _____

8. aeuplcef _____

9. clsecaocmip _____

10. senaemc _____

As you hear them, write the spelling words for the day in the space provided. Be sure that you correct any words you have spelled incorrectly.

1. _____

2. _____

3. _____

4. _____

5. _____

6. _____

7. _____

8. _____

9. _____

10. _____

11. _____

12. _____

13. _____

14. _____

15. _____

16. _____

17. _____

18. _____

19. _____

20. _____

21. _____

22. _____

23. _____

24. _____

25. _____

Using Your Words:

Sound alike words:

peace/piece

Circle the correct word in the sentences below:

1. May I have another (piece, peace) of cake?

2. Mr. Smith was cited by the police for disturbing the (piece, peace).

3. Let's try to (piece, peace) this quilt together before you leave.

4. The dove is the universal sign of (piece, peace).

Day 32

Spelling Lesson:

As you hear them, write the spelling words for the day in the space provided. Be sure that you correct any words you have spelled incorrectly.

1. _____

2. _____

3. _____

4. _____

5. _____

6. _____

7. _____

8. _____

9. _____

10. _____

11. _____

12. _____

13. _____

14. _____

15. _____

16. _____

17. _____

18. _____

19. _____

20. _____

21. _____

22. _____

23. _____

24. _____

25. _____

Using Your Words:

Choose seven words from your spelling list and use each of them in a sentence.

1._____

_____

2._____

_____

3._____

_____

4._____

_____

5._____

_____

6._____

_____

7._____

_____

Day 33

As you hear them, write the spelling words for the day in the space provided. Be sure that you correct any words you have spelled incorrectly.

1. _____

2. _____

3. _____

4. _____

5. _____

6. _____

7. _____

8. _____

9. _____

10. _____

11. _____

12. _____

13. _____

14. _____

15. _____

16. _____

17. _____

18. _____

19._____

20. _____

21. _____

22. _____

23. _____

24. _____

25. _____

Using Your Words:

Sound alike words

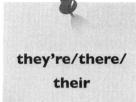

they're/there/their

Remember: **They're** means "they are."
Their is the possessive form of they.
There refers to a place.

Circle the correct word in the following sentences.

1. They always take (they're, there, their) dog with them on vacation.

2. Let's wait (they're, there, their) alongside the entrance to the mall.

3. When you talk to them, ask if (they're, there, their) coming tomorrow.

4. (They're, There, Their) football team is going to the state championship game.

5. Dad was pleased that they had done so well on (they're, there, their) ACT tests.

6. Her parents won't be joining us as (they're, there, their) both working that day.

7. Jack is always (they're, there, their) on time.

8. (They're, There, Their) leaving for the airport at 12:30 today.

Spelling Lesson:

As you hear them, write the spelling words for the day in the space provided. Be sure that you correct any words you have spelled incorrectly.

1. _____

2. _____

3. _____

4. _____

5. _____

6. _____

7. _____

8. _____

9. _____

10. _____

11. _____

12. _____

13. _____

14. _____

15. _____

16. _____

17. _____

18. _____

19. _____

20. _____

21. _____

22. _____

23. _____

24. _____

25. _____

Using Your Words:

Make as many words as you can from the following word: 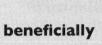 **beneficially**

Day 35

Spelling Lesson:

As you hear them, write the spelling words for the day in the space provided. Be sure that you correct any words you have spelled incorrectly.

1. _____
2. _____
3. _____
4. _____
5. _____
6. _____
7. _____
8. _____
9. _____
10. _____
11. _____
12. _____
13. _____

14. _____
15. _____
16. _____
17. _____
18. _____
19. _____
20. _____
21. _____
22. _____
23. _____
24. _____
25. _____

Using Your Words:

Unscramble these:

1. narhco _____

2. chtsoam _____

3. ircaal _____

4. lfiafoci _____

5. cjuiieldpar _____

6. uipisosusc _____

7. iceylommrlac _____

8. oowpincelam _____

9. rrocgey _____

10. sicedul _____

Day 36

Spelling Lesson:

As you hear them, write the spelling words for the day in the space provided. Be sure that you correct any words you have spelled incorrectly.

1. _____

2. _____

3. _____

4. _____

5. _____

6. _____

7. _____

8. _____

9. _____

10. _____

11. _____

12. _____

13. _____

14. _____

15. _____

16. _____

17. _____

18. _____

19. _____

20. _____

21. _____

22. _____

23. _____

24. _____

25. _____

Using Your Words:

Choose seven words from your spelling list and use each of them in a sentence.

1._____

_____

2._____

_____

3._____

_____

4._____

_____

5._____

_____

6._____

_____

7._____

_____

Spelling Lesson:

As you hear them, write the spelling words for the day in the space provided. Be sure that you correct any words you have spelled incorrectly.

1. _____

2. _____

3. _____

4. _____

5. _____

6. _____

7. _____

8. _____

9. _____

10. _____

11. _____

12. _____

13. _____

14. _____

15. _____

16. _____

17. _____

18. _____

19. _____

20. _____

21. _____

22. _____

23. _____

24. _____

25. _____

Using Your Words:

Choose seven words from your spelling list and use each of them in a sentence.

1._____

_____

2._____

_____

3._____

_____

4._____

_____

5._____

_____

6._____

_____

7._____

_____

Spelling Lesson:

As you hear them, write the spelling words for the day in the space provided. Be sure that you correct any words you have spelled incorrectly.

1. _____

2. _____

3. _____

4. _____

5. _____

6. _____

7. _____

8. _____

9. _____

10. _____

11. _____

12. _____

13. _____

14. _____

15. _____

16. _____

17. _____

18. _____

19. _____

20. _____

21. _____

22. _____

23. _____

24. _____

25. _____

Using Your Words:

Make as many words as you
can that have these letters
(in order).

ock

uck

Spelling Lesson:

As you hear them, write the spelling words for the day in the space provided. Be sure that you correct any words you have spelled incorrectly.

1. _____

2. _____

3. _____

4. _____

5. _____

6. _____

7. _____

8. _____

9. _____

10. _____

11. _____

12. _____

13. _____

14. _____

15. _____

16. _____

17. _____

18. _____

19. _____

20. _____

21. _____

22. _____

23. _____

24. _____

25. _____

Using Your Words:

Unscramble these:

1. ckyheo   _____

2. kcdroeedf   _____

3. dkcsohe   _____

4. uedkcd   _____

5. bdkuce   _____

6. lyukc   _____

7. edkncok   _____

8. ekcbdlo   _____

9. koccy   _____

10. dlkaoecpd   _____

Day 40

Spelling Lesson:

As you hear them, write the spelling words for the day in the space provided. Be sure that you correct any words you have spelled incorrectly.

1. _____

2. _____

3. _____

4. _____

5. _____

6. _____

7. _____

8. _____

9. _____

10. _____

11. _____

12. _____

13. _____

14. _____

15. _____

16. _____

17. _____

18. _____

19. _____

20. _____

21. _____

22. _____

23. _____

24. _____

25. _____

Using Your Words:

Can you **find** the words?

```
G N I K C U L C S R S N G D N
P W G C L X K A T R T N N T N
W C B S D E M S V W O T I R B
F P C Y A B E I B O C S K N R
D F D R D I S L L D K E C N G
H E X N K G O N E U I I O M A
R U R C R C A F U K N K M J N
A O U O K B R T S O G C E F E
B L C I H O G N I K C O L N U
Z Y N K C C S N S P L C Y Y L
O G X K I O N K I J B M P B E
V R I P E E R A K K X J H X S
K N F M O X S S H O C K I N G
G N A X R E C T H K R O Y Y R
Z C N W Q N B Z Y R P Q R S U
```

Words Used

anchored

blocking

cameos

clucking

cockiest

defrocking

luckiest

mocking

rockiest

rocking

shocking

stocking

unlocking

Evaluation Test #1

Fill in the blanks with the missing letters.

1. We have some unfin_____ business to attend to.

2. Every house should have a fire extingu_____.

3. Do you like bran muff_____?

4. You should try walking in another's moccas_____.

5. Would you like an en_____ level job?

6. The English brought star_____ to America.

7. Speakers love appl_____.

8. No one likes to be defr_____.

9. I wish you wouldn't be so part_____.

10. Famili_____ breeds contempt.

11. Please give at least one spec_____ example.

12. My older sister is an electri_____.

13. My older brother is a musi_____.

14. We told him not to panic, but he still panic_____ .

15. Afterwards, he was very apolog_____.

16. Have you not_____ how quickly you're learning?

17. A teacher spe_____izes in helping people learn.

18. It is cru_____ that you learn certain spelling concepts..

19. It will prove benefi_____ if you can master them.

20. Careful watching of commer_____ can help your reading.

Day 41

Spelling Lesson:

As you hear them, write the spelling words for the day in the space provided. Be sure that you correct any words you have spelled incorrectly.

1. _____

2. _____

3. _____

4. _____

5. _____

6. _____

7. _____

8. _____

9. _____

10. _____

11. _____

12. _____

13. _____

14. _____

15. _____

16. _____

17. _____

18. _____

19. _____

20. _____

21. _____

22. _____

23. _____

24. _____

25. _____

Using Your Words:

Fill in the blanks with words from today's spelling list.

1. The accident report said that the _____

   the car first.

2. Do you know what a _____ accelerator is?

3. Susan and Emily have the same _____ of friends.

4. My _____ taught me how to ride a _____

   when I was five.

5. After we finished digging out the shrubs in our yard, every _____ in my

   body ached,

6. The celebrations of the Millenium were quite a _____ .

7. The second _____ of the play was the longest.

Spelling Lesson:

As you hear them, write the spelling words for the day in the space provided. Be sure that you correct any words you have spelled incorrectly.

1. _____

2. _____

3. _____

4. _____

5. _____

6. _____

7. _____

8. _____

9. _____

10. _____

11. _____

12. _____

13. _____

14. _____

15. _____

16. _____

17. _____

18. _____

19. _____

20. _____

21. _____

22. _____

23. _____

24. _____

25. _____

Using Your Words:

Sound-alike words:

Use each of these correctly in a sentence.

**muscle/mussel
acts/ax/axe**

1._____

_____

2._____

_____

3._____

_____

4._____

_____

5._____

_____

Spelling Lesson:

As you hear them, write the spelling words for the day in the space provided. Be sure that you correct any words you have spelled incorrectly.

1. _____

2. _____

3. _____

4. _____

5. _____

6. _____

7. _____

8. _____

9. _____

10. _____

11. _____

12. _____

13. _____

14. _____

15. _____

16. _____

17. _____

18. _____

19. _____

20. _____

21. _____

22. _____

23. _____

24. _____

25. _____

Using Your Words:

Make as many words as you can from the letters in the following word.

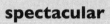 **spectacular**

_____

_____

_____

_____

_____

_____

_____

_____

_____

_____

Spelling Lesson:

As you hear them, write the spelling words for the day in the space provided. Be sure that you correct any words you have spelled incorrectly.

1. _____

2. _____

3. _____

4. _____

5. _____

6. _____

7. _____

8. _____

9. _____

10. _____

11. _____

12. _____

13. _____

14. _____

15. _____

16. _____

17. _____

18. _____

19. _____

20. _____

21. _____

22. _____

23. _____

24. _____

25. _____

Using Your Words:

Choose seven of the words in your spelling list and use each word in a sentence.

1._____

_____

2._____

_____

3._____

_____

4._____

_____

5._____

_____

6._____

_____

7._____

_____

Day 45

Spelling Lesson:

As you hear them, write the spelling words for the day in the space provided. Be sure that you correct any words you have spelled incorrectly.

1. _____

2. _____

3. _____

4. _____

5. _____

6. _____

7. _____

8. _____

9. _____

10. _____

11. _____

12. _____

13. _____

14. _____

15. _____

16. _____

17. _____

18. _____

19. _____

20. _____

21. _____

22. _____

23. _____

24. _____

25. _____

Using Your Words:

Sound alike words:

Use each of these in a sentence correctly.

pack/packed

tract/tracked

tact/tacked

1._____

_____

2._____

_____

3._____

_____

4._____

_____

5._____

_____

6._____

_____

7._____

_____

Spelling Lesson:

As you hear them, write the spelling words for the day in the space provided. Be sure that you correct any words you have spelled incorrectly.

1. _____

2. _____

3. _____

4. _____

5. _____

6. _____

7. _____

8. _____

9. _____

10. _____

11. _____

12. _____

13. _____

14. _____

15. _____

16. _____

17. _____

18. _____

19. _____

20. _____

21. _____

22. _____

23. _____

24. _____

25. _____

Using Your Words:

List as many words as you can with the following letters (in order) in them.

act

Spelling Lesson:

As you hear them, write the spelling words for the day in the space provided. Be sure that you correct any words you have spelled incorrectly.

1. _____

2. _____

3. _____

4. _____

5. _____

6. _____

7. _____

8. _____

9. _____

10. _____

11. _____

12. _____

13. _____

14. _____

15. _____

16. _____

17. _____

18. _____

19. _____

20. _____

21. _____

22. _____

23. _____

24. _____

25. _____

Using Your Words:

Unscramble these:

1. rntcataito   _____

2. ubntagtcris   _____

3. detrcancot   _____

4. itccnonrtoa   _____

5. itepdacm   _____

6. caattrac   _____

7. lrrcsaatlhaiyecti _____

8. rdteaufcr   _____

9. atcict   _____

10. rtatorc   _____

Spelling Lesson:

As you hear them, write the spelling words for the day in the space provided. Be sure that you correct any words you have spelled incorrectly.

1. _____

2. _____

3. _____

4. _____

5. _____

6. _____

7. _____

8. _____

9. _____

10. _____

11. _____

12. _____

13. _____

14. _____

15. _____

16. _____

17. _____

18. _____

19. _____

20. _____

21. _____

22. _____

23. _____

24. _____

25. _____

Using Your Words:

Choose seven words from your spelling list and use each of them correctly in a sentence.

1._____

_____

2._____

_____

3._____

_____

4._____

_____

5._____

_____

6._____

_____

7._____

_____

Sequential Spelling Level 4 - Student Workbook

Spelling Lesson:

As you hear them, write the spelling words for the day in the space provided. Be sure that you correct any words you have spelled incorrectly.

1. _____

2. _____

3. _____

4. _____

5. _____

6. _____

7. _____

8. _____

9. _____

10. _____

11. _____

12. _____

13. _____

14. _____

15. _____

16. _____

17. _____

18. _____

19. _____

20. _____

21. _____

22. _____

23. _____

24. _____

25. _____

Using Your Words:

Tricky Words:.

Affect means to have an effect on or influence.

Effect means result or fulfillment.

Circle the correct word to complete each sentence.

1. This quiz will have no (affect, effect) on our final grade for the class.

2. I didn't expect that movie to (affect, effect) me the way it did.

3. Don't let those comments (affect, effect) you.

4. Allison likes the (affect, effect) of the color wash on her painting.

5. Skipping class regularly will have an (affect, effect) on your grades.

6. Our new rules are having the desired (affect, effect).

7. What (affect, effect) do you think the news will have?

8. No matter what the final decision is, it won't (affect, effect) me.

Day 50

Spelling Lesson:

As you hear them, write the spelling words for the day in the space provided. Be sure that you correct any words you have spelled incorrectly.

1. _____

2. _____

3. _____

4. _____

5. _____

6. _____

7. _____

8. _____

9. _____

10. _____

11. _____

12. _____

13. _____

14. _____

15. _____

16. _____

17. _____

18. _____

19. _____

20. _____

21. _____

22. _____

23. _____

24. _____

25. _____

Using Your Words:

Look alike words

Use each of these correctly
in a sentence

object "ub JEK't"/
object "AH'b jekt"

subject "sub JEK't/
subject "SUB jekt"

perfect "pur FEK't"

project "proh JEK't"/
project "PRAH jekt"

1._____

_____

2._____

_____

3._____

_____

4._____

_____

5._____

_____

6._____

_____

7._____

_____

Sequential Spelling Level 4 - Student Workbook

Day 51

As you hear them, write the spelling words for the day in the space provided. Be sure that you correct any words you have spelled incorrectly.

1. _____

2. _____

3. _____

4. _____

5. _____

6. _____

7. _____

8. _____

9. _____

10. _____

11. _____

12. _____

13. _____

14. _____

15. _____

16. _____

17. _____

18. _____

19. _____

20. _____

21. _____

22. _____

23. _____

24. _____

25. _____

Using Your Words:

List as many words as you can that have the following letters (in order) in them:

ive

ect

_____

_____

_____

_____

_____

_____

_____

_____

_____

_____

_____

_____

Day 52

Spelling Lesson:

As you hear them, write the spelling words for the day in the space provided. Be sure that you correct any words you have spelled incorrectly.

1. _____

2. _____

3. _____

4. _____

5. _____

6. _____

7. _____

8. _____

9. _____

10. _____

11. _____

12. _____

13. _____

14. _____

15. _____

16. _____

17. _____

18. _____

19. _____

20. _____

21. _____

22. _____

23. _____

24. _____

25. _____

Using Your Words:

Can you find the words?

```
R M X N H S P H A J S B N U J
P M Y Y O W C F Z N G O O Z Q
B E X L R I F E O H I M I X B
A U R R E E T I L T Y D T Y L
X Z E F C V T C C L E M C L G
J O P T E C I E E D O I E E N
C Z I D E C L T A J E P J V E
G O A R L E T J C N E V B I G
N P I I S Q T I E E W R O T L
F D Q U K W I I O E J Q Y C E
N O I T C E F N I N U B G E C
E R E C T I N G C O C A O F T
B I F O X O P R E D T U J F I
E C N E G I L L E T N I I E N
F K T S C O R R E C T I O N G
```

Words Used

affection

cello

correction

directions

effectively

erecting

infection

intelligence

neglecting

objection

objectively

perfection

rejection

selection

Sequential Spelling Level 4 - Student Workbook

Day 53

Spelling Lesson:

As you hear them, write the spelling words for the day in the space provided. Be sure that you correct any words you have spelled incorrectly.

1. _____

2. _____

3. _____

4. _____

5. _____

6. _____

7. _____

8. _____

9. _____

10. _____

11. _____

12. _____

13. _____

14. _____

15. _____

16. _____

17. _____

18. _____

19. _____

20. _____

21. _____

22. _____

23. _____

24. _____

25. _____

Using Your Words:

Make as many words as
you can from the
letters in the word:

prospector

Spelling Lesson:

As you hear them, write the spelling words for the day in the space provided. Be sure that you correct any words you have spelled incorrectly.

1. _____

2. _____

3. _____

4. _____

5. _____

6. _____

7. _____

8. _____

9. _____

10. _____

11. _____

12. _____

13. _____

14. _____

15. _____

16. _____

17. _____

18. _____

19. _____

20. _____

21. _____

22. _____

23. _____

24. _____

25. _____

Using Your Words:

Choose seven of your spelling words and use each of them correctly in a sentence.

1._____

_____

2._____

_____

3._____

_____

4._____

_____

5._____

_____

6._____

_____

7._____

_____

Day 55

As you hear them, write the spelling words for the day in the space provided. Be sure that you correct any words you have spelled incorrectly.

1. _____

2. _____

3. _____

4. _____

5. _____

6. _____

7. _____

8. _____

9. _____

10. _____

11. _____

12. _____

13. _____

14. _____

15. _____

16. _____

17. _____

18. _____

19. _____

20. _____

21. _____

22. _____

23. _____

24. _____

25. _____

Using Your Words:

Unscramble these:

1. cxepdete   _____

2. unedpetxec   _____

3. isstcen   _____

4. tcutcraerehi   _____

5. ileyeactllrc   _____

6. uelcdetr   _____

7. icusonspi   _____

8. iflgntueegcn   _____

9. cnsusiiop   _____

10. spsetduce   _____

As you hear them, write the spelling words for the day in the space provided. Be sure that you correct any words you have spelled incorrectly.

1. _____
2. _____
3. _____
4. _____
5. _____
6. _____
7. _____
8. _____
9. _____
10. _____
11. _____
12. _____
13. _____

14. _____
15. _____
16. _____
17. _____
18. _____
19. _____
20. _____
21. _____
22. _____
23. _____
24. _____
25. _____

Using Your Words:

Use a dictionary to find the meanings of these spelling words and then use them in a sentence.

1. expectations _____

_____

2. dissection _____

_____

3. bisection _____

_____

4. intersection _____

_____

5. imperfect _____

_____

6. genuflection _____

_____

7. suspect _____

_____

8. reflection _____

_____

Day 57

As you hear them, write the spelling words for the day in the space provided. Be sure that you correct any words you have spelled incorrectly.

1. _____

2. _____

3. _____

4. _____

5. _____

6. _____

7. _____

8. _____

9. _____

10. _____

11. _____

12. _____

13. _____

14. _____

15. _____

16. _____

17. _____

18. _____

19. _____

20. _____

21. _____

22. _____

23. _____

24. _____

25. _____

Using Your Words:

List as many words as you can which have the following letters (in order) in them.

ict

_____

_____

_____

_____

_____

_____

_____

_____

_____

_____

Day 58

Spelling Lesson:

As you hear them, write the spelling words for the day in the space provided. Be sure that you correct any words you have spelled incorrectly.

1. _____

2. _____

3. _____

4. _____

5. _____

6. _____

7. _____

8. _____

9. _____

10. _____

11. _____

12. _____

13. _____

14. _____

15. _____

16. _____

17. _____

18. _____

19. _____

20. _____

21. _____

22. _____

23. _____

24. _____

25. _____

Using Your Words:

Use a dictionary to find the meanings of these words. Then, use each word in a sentence.

1. interdict _____

_____

2. derelict _____

_____

3. indict _____

_____

4. concoct _____

_____

5. proctor _____

_____

Spelling Lesson:

As you hear them, write the spelling words for the day in the space provided. Be sure that you correct any words you have spelled incorrectly.

1. _____

2. _____

3. _____

4. _____

5. _____

6. _____

7. _____

8. _____

9. _____

10. _____

11. _____

12. _____

13. _____

14. _____

15. _____

16. _____

17. _____

18. _____

19. _____

20. _____

21. _____

22. _____

23. _____

24. _____

25. _____

Using Your Words:

Unscramble these:

1. dtecidda _____

2. vyritoc _____

3. ocioncnitartd _____

4. ecbinienotd _____

5. soitcitnrre _____

6. decinttidre _____

7. cntoodecc _____

8. drcoterpo _____

9. roocddte _____

10. gphticni _____

Day 60

Spelling Lesson:

As you hear them, write the spelling words for the day in the space provided. Be sure that you correct any words you have spelled incorrectly.

1. _____

2. _____

3. _____

4. _____

5. _____

6. _____

7. _____

8. _____

9. _____

10. _____

11. _____

12. _____

13. _____

14. _____

15. _____

16. _____

17. _____

18. _____

19. _____

20. _____

21. _____

22. _____

23. _____

24. _____

25. _____

Using Your Words:

Choose seven of your spelling words and use each of them correctly in a sentence.

1._____

_____

2._____

_____

3._____

_____

4._____

_____

5._____

_____

6._____

_____

7._____

_____

Day 61

Spelling Lesson:

As you hear them, write the spelling words for the day in the space provided. Be sure that you correct any words you have spelled incorrectly.

1. _____

2. _____

3. _____

4. _____

5. _____

6. _____

7. _____

8. _____

9. _____

10. _____

11. _____

12. _____

13. _____

14. _____

15. _____

16. _____

17. _____

18. _____

19. _____

20. _____

21. _____

22. _____

23. _____

24. _____

25. _____

Using Your Words:

Sound alike words:

Find the meanings of the words that you don't know. Then, use each word in a sentence.

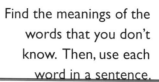
duct/ducked

ducts/ducks

1._____

_____

2._____

_____

3._____

_____

4._____

_____

Day 62

Spelling Lesson:

As you hear them, write the spelling words for the day in the space provided. Be sure that you correct any words you have spelled incorrectly.

1. _____   14. _____

2. _____   15. _____

3. _____   16. _____

4. _____   17. _____

5. _____   18. _____

6. _____   19. _____

7. _____   20. _____

8. _____   21. _____

9. _____   22. _____

10. _____   23. _____

11. _____   24. _____

12. _____   25. _____

13. _____

Using Your Words:

Make as many words
as you can from the
following word:

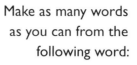

conductor

_____

_____

_____

_____

_____

_____

_____

_____

_____

_____

_____

_____

_____

_____

_____

_____

_____

As you hear them, write the spelling words for the day in the space provided. Be sure that you correct any words you have spelled incorrectly.

1. _____

2. _____

3. _____

4. _____

5. _____

6. _____

7. _____

8. _____

9. _____

10. _____

11. _____

12. _____

13. _____

14. _____

15. _____

16. _____

17. _____

18. _____

19. _____

20. _____

21. _____

22. _____

23. _____

24. _____

25. _____

Using Your Words:

Fill in the blank with words from today's spelling list.

1. The flight attendants _____ us to use the oxygen

   masks if the airplane's cabin lost pressure.

2. Are you more _____ in the morning or afternoon?

3. Sam _____ on his paper while he waiting for his dad

   to pick him up.

4. We watched as Mr. Smith _____ the science experiment.

5. While riding our bikes, we discovered that a house was being _____

   on the vacant lot on Pine Street.

6. _____ criticism is a good thing.

7. _____ you rather have lemonade?

8. Do you think Susan_____ that we wanted to meet her at noon?

Spelling Lesson:

As you hear them, write the spelling words for the day in the space provided. Be sure that you correct any words you have spelled incorrectly.

1. _____

2. _____

3. _____

4. _____

5. _____

6. _____

7. _____

8. _____

9. _____

10. _____

11. _____

12. _____

13. _____

14. _____

15. _____

16. _____

17. _____

18. _____

19. _____

20. _____

21. _____

22. _____

23. _____

24. _____

25. _____

Using Your Words:

Can You find the Words?

```
E  T  C  S  E  L  D  O  O  P  U  S  N  F  S
I  D  O  G  J  H  Q  J  F  H  C  O  Y  Z  T
Q  N  N  S  M  X  K  P  F  F  I  F  F  K  W
M  I  S  U  N  D  E  R  S  T  O  O  D  Y  O
G  N  T  T  N  O  I  T  C  U  D  O  R  P  O
N  X  R  V  R  K  I  U  D  D  C  O  V  B  D
I  N  U  R  I  U  D  T  E  O  F  R  S  R  E
T  H  C  P  D  B  C  D  C  S  O  T  C  V  N
C  C  T  F  A  O  U  T  S  U  R  W  U  B  L
U  B  I  O  J  C  O  B  I  U  D  B  G  S  Y
D  U  O  M  I  B  B  D  C  O  O  E  V  O  I
N  S  N  N  V  S  T  T  L  G  N  Y  D  X  D
O  P  G  U  R  Y  I  V  A  E  F  S  X  P  J
C  S  C  P  R  O  D  U  C  E  R  S  G  U  G
B  W  P  F  N  M  A  I  V  K  Z  S  J  C  W
```

Words Used

abduction

conducting

construction

deducing

deductions

dogwood

doodlers

instructions

misunderstood

obstruction

poodles

producers

production

woodenly

Day 65

Spelling Lesson:

As you hear them, write the spelling words for the day in the space provided. Be sure that you correct any words you have spelled incorrectly.

1. _____

2. _____

3. _____

4. _____

5. _____

6. _____

7. _____

8. _____

9. _____

10. _____

11. _____

12. _____

13. _____

14. _____

15. _____

16. _____

17. _____

18. _____

19. _____

20. _____

21. _____

22. _____

23. _____

24. _____

25. _____

Using Your Words:

List as many words as you can that have the following letters (in order) in them.

hood

Spelling Lesson:

As you hear them, write the spelling words for the day in the space provided. Be sure that you correct any words you have spelled incorrectly.

1. _____

2. _____

3. _____

4. _____

5. _____

6. _____

7. _____

8. _____

9. _____

10. _____

11. _____

12. _____

13. _____

14. _____

15. _____

16. _____

17. _____

18. _____

19. _____

20. _____

21. _____

22. _____

23. _____

24. _____

25. _____

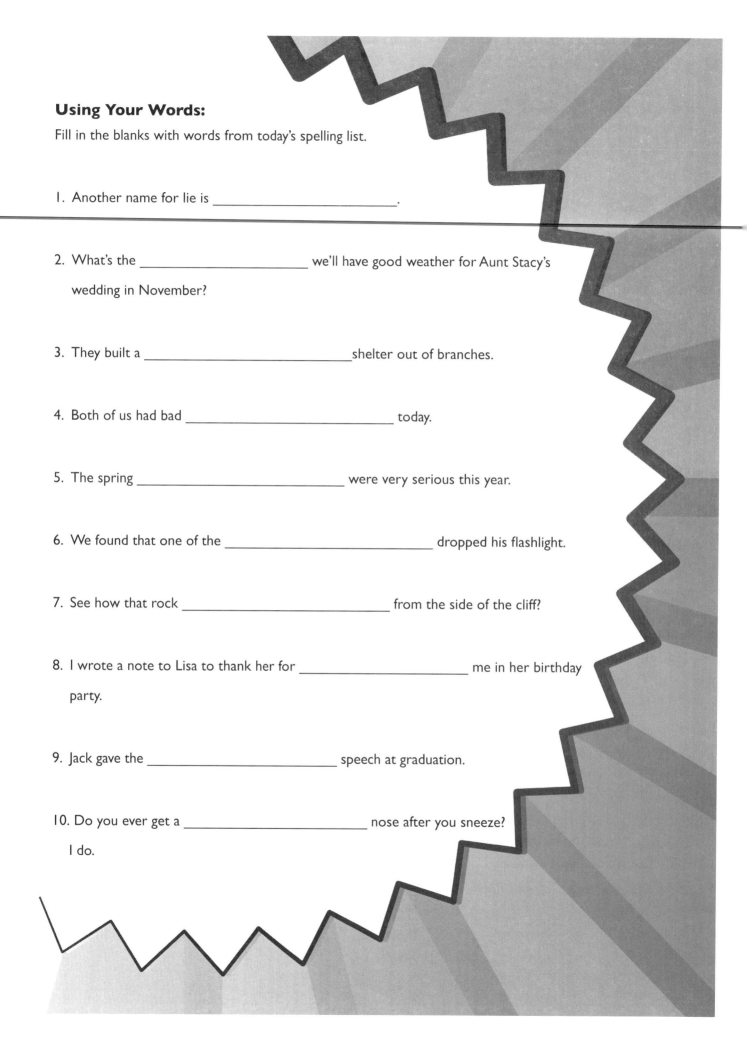

Using Your Words:

Fill in the blanks with words from today's spelling list.

1. Another name for lie is _____.

2. What's the _____ we'll have good weather for Aunt Stacy's wedding in November?

3. They built a _____ shelter out of branches.

4. Both of us had bad _____ today.

5. The spring _____ were very serious this year.

6. We found that one of the _____ dropped his flashlight.

7. See how that rock _____ from the side of the cliff?

8. I wrote a note to Lisa to thank her for _____ me in her birthday party.

9. Jack gave the _____ speech at graduation.

10. Do you ever get a _____ nose after you sneeze? I do.

Spelling Lesson:

As you hear them, write the spelling words for the day in the space provided. Be sure that you correct any words you have spelled incorrectly.

1. _____

2. _____

3. _____

4. _____

5. _____

6. _____

7. _____

8. _____

9. _____

10. _____

11. _____

12. _____

13. _____

14. _____

15. _____

16. _____

17. _____

18. _____

19. _____

20. _____

21. _____

22. _____

23. _____

24. _____

25. _____

Using Your Words:

Tricky Words:
Allude is a verb which means to refer indirectly.
Elude is a verb which means to escape or avoid.

Allude

Elude

Circle the correct word in each sentence.

1. In his acceptance speech, Jack (alluded, eluded) to his high school drama teacher.

2. The burglar (alluded, eluded) detection and escaped.

3. The solution to this problem (alludes, eludes) me.

4. Do you think the reference in the book (alludes, eludes) to his time in Spain?

5. There was something I wanted to tell you, but it's (alluding, eluding) me at the moment.

6. We didn't want to bring up the problem directly, but we tried to (allude, elude) to it so we could talk about it.

Spelling Lesson:

As you hear them, write the spelling words for the day in the space provided. Be sure that you correct any words you have spelled incorrectly.

1. _____

2. _____

3. _____

4. _____

5. _____

6. _____

7. _____

8. _____

9. _____

10. _____

11. _____

12. _____

13. _____

14. _____

15. _____

16. _____

17. _____

18. _____

19. _____

20. _____

21. _____

22. _____

23. _____

24. _____

25. _____

Using Your Words:

Unscramble these:

1. dlfignoo _____

2. lonilsiu _____

3. lndiuseo _____

4. onuloisccn _____

5. otheorhdom _____

6. obenrohdosgih _____

7. pdrmiay _____

8. ldigeun _____

9. snllouia _____

10. cnsinouii _____

141

Spelling Lesson:

As you hear them, write the spelling words for the day in the space provided. Be sure that you correct any words you have spelled incorrectly.

1. _____

2. _____

3. _____

4. _____

5. _____

6. _____

7. _____

8. _____

9. _____

10. _____

11. _____

12. _____

13. _____

14. _____

15. _____

16. _____

17. _____

18. _____

19. _____

20. _____

21. _____

22. _____

23. _____

24. _____

25. _____

Using Your Words:

List as many words as you can with the following letters (in order) in them:

alm

eign

Spelling Lesson:

As you hear them, write the spelling words for the day in the space provided. Be sure that you correct any words you have spelled incorrectly.

1. _____

2. _____

3. _____

4. _____

5. _____

6. _____

7. _____

8. _____

9. _____

10. _____

11. _____

12. _____

13. _____

14. _____

15. _____

16. _____

17. _____

18. _____

19. _____

20. _____

21. _____

22. _____

23. _____

24. _____

25. _____

Using Your Words:

Sound alike words:

Use a dictionary to find the meanings of the words you don't know; then use each of them correctly in a sentence.

rain/rein/reign
sign/sine
gnu/new/knew

1. _____

_____

2. _____

_____

3. _____

_____

4. _____

_____

5. _____

_____

6. _____

_____

7. _____

_____

8. _____

_____

Spelling Lesson:

As you hear them, write the spelling words for the day in the space provided. Be sure that you correct any words you have spelled incorrectly.

1. _____
2. _____
3. _____
4. _____
5. _____
6. _____
7. _____
8. _____
9. _____
10. _____
11. _____
12. _____
13. _____

14. _____
15. _____
16. _____
17. _____
18. _____
19. _____
20. _____
21. _____
22. _____
23. _____
24. _____
25. _____

Using your words:

Unscramble these:

1. sutregian   _____

2. iadneogtsni   _____

3. nug   _____

4. ieergrnosf   _____

5. ecldma   _____

6. masnol   _____

7. ottseonmb   _____

8. blam   _____

9. brmoeb   _____

10. iagtmnaln   _____

Spelling Lesson:

As you hear them, write the spelling words for the day in the space provided. Be sure that you correct any words you have spelled incorrectly.

1. _____

2. _____

3. _____

4. _____

5. _____

6. _____

7. _____

8. _____

9. _____

10. _____

11. _____

12. _____

13. _____

14. _____

15. _____

16. _____

17. _____

18. _____

19. _____

20. _____

21. _____

22. _____

23. _____

24. _____

25. _____

Using Your Words:

Choose seven words from today's spelling list and use each in a sentence.

1._____

_____

2._____

_____

3._____

_____

4._____

_____

5._____

_____

6._____

_____

7._____

_____

Day 73

Spelling Lesson:

As you hear them, write the spelling words for the day in the space provided. Be sure that you correct any words you have spelled incorrectly.

1. _____

2. _____

3. _____

4. _____

5. _____

6. _____

7. _____

8. _____

9. _____

10. _____

11. _____

12. _____

13. _____

14. _____

15. _____

16. _____

17. _____

18. _____

19. _____

20. _____

21. _____

22. _____

23. _____

24. _____

25. _____

Using Your Words:

Sound alike words:

Find the meanings of the words that you don't know. Then, use each word in a sentence

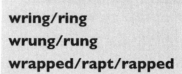

**wring/ring
wrung/rung
wrapped/rapt/rapped**

1._____

_____

2._____

_____

3._____

_____

4._____

_____

5._____

_____

6._____

_____

7._____

_____

Spelling Lesson:

As you hear them, write the spelling words for the day in the space provided. Be sure that you correct any words you have spelled incorrectly.

1. _____

2. _____

3. _____

4. _____

5. _____

6. _____

7. _____

8. _____

9. _____

10. _____

11. _____

12. _____

13. _____

14. _____

15. _____

16. _____

17. _____

18. _____

19. _____

20. _____

21. _____

22. _____

23. _____

24. _____

25. _____

Using Your Words:

Unscramble these:

1. nwesrkli _____

2. twersslre _____

3. risrtew _____

4. erhwtis _____

5. rwdoss _____

6. terhwas _____

7. hwftrula _____

8. creneswh _____

9. secrsae _____

10. rsnwsae _____

Day 75

As you hear them, write the spelling words for the day in the space provided. Be sure that you correct any words you have spelled incorrectly.

1. _____

2. _____

3. _____

4. _____

5. _____

6. _____

7. _____

8. _____

9. _____

10. _____

11. _____

12. _____

13. _____

14. _____

15. _____

16. _____

17. _____

18. _____

19. _____

20. _____

21. _____

22. _____

23. _____

24. _____

25. _____

Using Your Words:

Circle the correct answer.

1. (Who's, Whose) going to choose the decorations for the party?

2. (Who's, Whose) left foot is bigger? Yours or mine?

3. I'm not sure (who's, whose) house we're going to first.

4. (Who's, Whose) the new student?

5. Do you know (who's, whose) books are on the table?

6. I can't remember (who's, whose) bike I borrowed last week.

7. (Who's, Whose) running in the 10k this Saturday?

8. (Who's, Whose) bringing the fruit for the smoothies we're making?

Day 76

Spelling Lesson:

As you hear them, write the spelling words for the day in the space provided. Be sure that you correct any words you have spelled incorrectly.

1. _____

2. _____

3. _____

4. _____

5. _____

6. _____

7. _____

8. _____

9. _____

10. _____

11. _____

12. _____

13. _____

14. _____

15. _____

16. _____

17. _____

18. _____

19. _____

20. _____

21. _____

22. _____

23. _____

24. _____

25. _____

Using Your Words:

Can You  The Words?

```
I M X S E O W N H R O C G K G
W H C W D Y F R E Y G N S V N
R L T O Q Z L L I H I T D B I
A S P R Y G E R C G S D M Q L
P W R D I A N L N I M D D Q K
P J R F S G N I R E W S N A N
I H H I S W R W H W M G T V I
N D N G T W G B I C O A N G R
G G U H Q H L N O C N S R N W
O S P T G N I T I R W E X N Y
W R O N G S X N T S A I R V L
H U Z W J K S Y G S A O S W L
D E C E A S E D I O U E L G O
P V D A B D A N D T J S L Z H
K A I T Q Z G T X B F O E P W
```

Words Used

answering

deceased

greasing

leasing

releasing

swordfight

wholly

wrapping

wrenching

wringing

wrinkling

wrists

writhing

writing

wrongs

Spelling Lesson:

As you hear them, write the spelling words for the day in the space provided. Be sure that you correct any words you have spelled incorrectly.

1. _____

2. _____

3. _____

4. _____

5. _____

6. _____

7. _____

8. _____

9. _____

10. _____

11. _____

12. _____

13. _____

14. _____

15. _____

16. _____

17. _____

18. _____

19. _____

20. _____

21. _____

22. _____

23. _____

24. _____

25. _____

Using Your Words:

Make as many words as you can with the following letters (in order) in them.

eaters

_____

_____

_____

_____

_____

_____

_____

_____

_____

_____

Day 78

Spelling Lesson:

As you hear them, write the spelling words for the day in the space provided. Be sure that you correct any words you have spelled incorrectly.

1. _____

2. _____

3. _____

4. _____

5. _____

6. _____

7. _____

8. _____

9. _____

10. _____

11. _____

12. _____

13. _____

14. _____

15. _____

16. _____

17. _____

18. _____

19. _____

20. _____

21. _____

22. _____

23. _____

24. _____

25. _____

Using your words:

Unscramble these:

1. tghhwsievaye _____

2. byafolvar _____

3. rfaluosv _____

4. ecreisve _____

5. esvale _____

6. rsabveee _____

7. eevssel _____

8. ervehia _____

9. vrelcsae _____

10. aednfe _____

Day 79

Spelling Lesson:

As you hear them, write the spelling words for the day in the space provided. Be sure that you correct any words you have spelled incorrectly.

1. _____

2. _____

3. _____

4. _____

5. _____

6. _____

7. _____

8. _____

9. _____

10. _____

11. _____

12. _____

13. _____

14. _____

15. _____

16. _____

17. _____

18. _____

19. _____

20. _____

21. _____

22. _____

23. _____

24. _____

25. _____

Using Your Words

Choose the correct answer.

1. According to legend, (they're, their, there) is buried treasure on the island.

2. Gram and Gramps just called to tell us (they're, their, there) coming for a visit this week.

3. I can't wait to see the looks on (they're, their, there) faces when I bring Jack to the party!

4. Do you know if (they're, their, there) planning to go to the movies with us?

5. I'm going to stay out of the discussion since it's (they're, their, there) decision.

6. I think Emily left her glasses over (they're, their, there).

7. They haven't called yet. I wonder if (they're, their, there) home yet.

8. (They're, Their, There) is a snake in my basket!

Day 80

Spelling Lesson:

As you hear them, write the spelling words for the day in the space provided. Be sure that you correct any words you have spelled incorrectly.

1. _____

2. _____

3. _____

4. _____

5. _____

6. _____

7. _____

8. _____

9. _____

10. _____

11. _____

12. _____

13. _____

14. _____

15. _____

16. _____

17. _____

18. _____

19. _____

20. _____

21. _____

22. _____

23. _____

24. _____

25. _____

Using Your Words

Choose seven of your spelling words and use them in a short paragraph, silly story or poem.

1. _____

_____

2. _____

_____

3. _____

_____

4. _____

_____

5. _____

_____

6. _____

_____

7. _____

_____

Sequential Spelling Level 4 - Student Workbook

Evaluation Test #2

Fill in the blanks with the missing letters.

1. It would be a mir_____if Chicago won the series.

2. The patient made a mirac_____ recovery.

3. The two countries signed a non-aggression p_____.

4. Sugar attr_____. ants.

5. Do you like previews of coming attr_____ ?

6. We stand corr_____ .

7. Do you need dir_____ on how to get there?.

8. You really should wear prot_____ headgear.

9. We attended three l_____ last year.

10. That patient is on a restr_____ diet.

11. How many of the psychic's pred_____ came true?

12. How many heat d_____ are there in this room?

13. My brother works for a constr_____ company.

14. I think my sister has a real attit_____ problem.

15. How do you think I arrived at that concl_____ ?

16. What would you like inscribed on your t_____ stone?

17. Have you seen the latest house des_____ ?

18. Our national debt seems to keep incr_____.

19. I don't like to be threat_____ by anyone.

20. We gave them new sw_____ for their anniversary.

Day 81

Spelling Lesson:

As you hear them, write the spelling words for the day in the space provided. Be sure that you correct any words you have spelled incorrectly.

1. _____

2. _____

3. _____

4. _____

5. _____

6. _____

7. _____

8. _____

9. _____

10. _____

11. _____

12. _____

13. _____

14. _____

15. _____

16. _____

17. _____

18. _____

19. _____

20. _____

21. _____

22. _____

23. _____

24. _____

25. _____

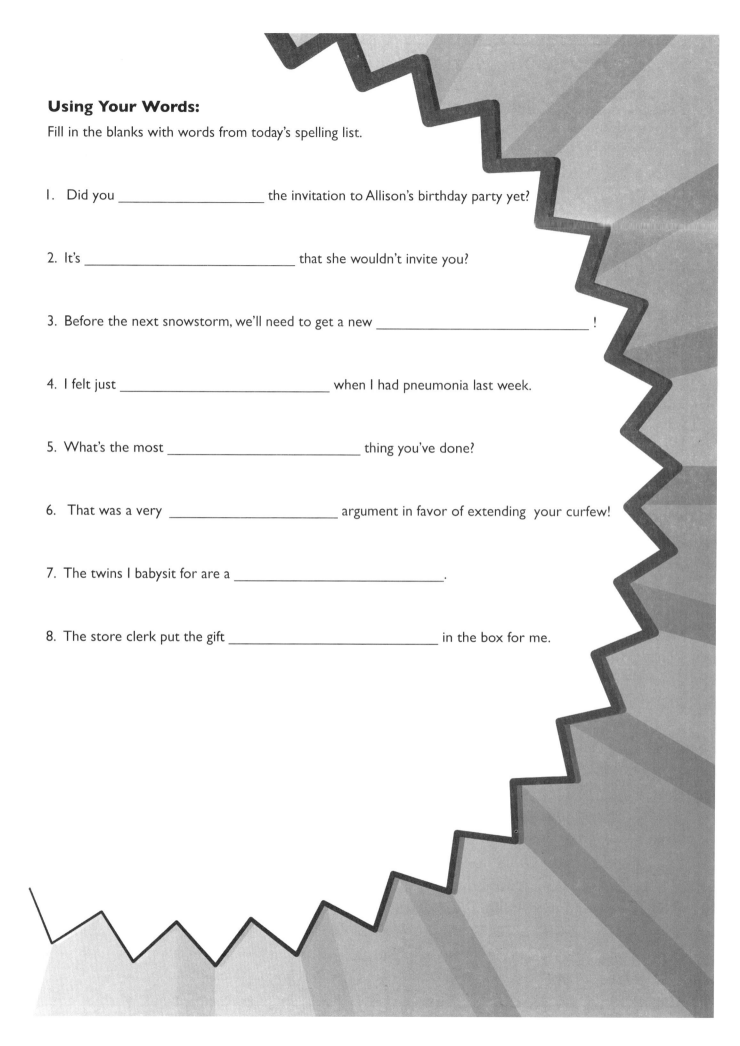

Using Your Words:

Fill in the blanks with words from today's spelling list.

1. Did you _____ the invitation to Allison's birthday party yet?

2. It's _____ that she wouldn't invite you?

3. Before the next snowstorm, we'll need to get a new _____ !

4. I felt just _____ when I had pneumonia last week.

5. What's the most _____ thing you've done?

6. That was a very _____ argument in favor of extending your curfew!

7. The twins I babysit for are a _____.

8. The store clerk put the gift _____ in the box for me.

Spelling Lesson:

As you hear them, write the spelling words for the day in the space provided. Be sure that you correct any words you have spelled incorrectly.

1. _____

2. _____

3. _____

4. _____

5. _____

6. _____

7. _____

8. _____

9. _____

10. _____

11. _____

12. _____

13. _____

14. _____

15. _____

16. _____

17. _____

18. _____

19. _____

20. _____

21. _____

22. _____

23. _____

24. _____

25. _____

Using Your Words:

Make as many words as
you can from the letters
in the following word:

dreadfully

Day 83

Spelling Lesson:

As you hear them, write the spelling words for the day in the space provided. Be sure that you correct any words you have spelled incorrectly.

1. _____

2. _____

3. _____

4. _____

5. _____

6. _____

7. _____

8. _____

9. _____

10. _____

11. _____

12. _____

13. _____

14. _____

15. _____

16. _____

17. _____

18. _____

19. _____

20. _____

21. _____

22. _____

23. _____

24. _____

25. _____

Using Your Words:

Unscramble these:

1. ldesevhol _____

2. pucealfe _____

3. fluyee _____

4. thouulfm _____

5. eecropvecind _____

6. ptceivere _____

7. vecedied _____

8. inilgec _____

9. elhlsrvdie _____

10. glfluee _____

Day 84

As you hear them, write the spelling words for the day in the space provided. Be sure that you correct any words you have spelled incorrectly.

1. _____

2. _____

3. _____

4. _____

5. _____

6. _____

7. _____

8. _____

9. _____

10. _____

11. _____

12. _____

13. _____

14. _____

15. _____

16. _____

17. _____

18. _____

19. _____

20. _____

21. _____

22. _____

23. _____

24. _____

25. _____

Using Your Words:

Can you find the Words?

G M G C V Y D R I I G I B S I
N O R L N L R E H N M M H N E
I U O J U L E E I I H O O W A
L T V R Q U B V V Q V I F X S
E H E Z Z F I H N E T T D P P
V F L R N E J P L P L V S X O
I U E X C C H E E J E I Q X O
R L D E R R D C F W F R N L N
H S R U X U N I M S E U O G F
S M I S C O N C E P T I O N U
K S W U C S W I V E L I N G L
U Q U E W E N O V E L T I E S
Y B R I G R N O I T P E C E R
A P Y L L U F E C A E P J Y C
V H I U K V F T V S J I N V U

Words Used

groveled

misconception

mouthfuls

novelties

peacefully

preconception

receiving

reception

resourcefully

reveling

shoveled

shriveling

swiveling

teaspoonfuls

Day 85

Spelling Lesson:

As you hear them, write the spelling words for the day in the space provided. Be sure that you correct any words you have spelled incorrectly.

1. _____

2. _____

3. _____

4. _____

5. _____

6. _____

7. _____

8. _____

9. _____

10. _____

11. _____

12. _____

13. _____

14. _____

15. _____

16. _____

17. _____

18. _____

19. _____

20. _____

21. _____

22. _____

23. _____

24. _____

25. _____

Using Your Words:

List as many words as
you can which have
the following letters
(in order) in them.

eerful

_____

_____

_____

_____

_____

_____

_____

_____

_____

Spelling Lesson:

As you hear them, write the spelling words for the day in the space provided. Be sure that you correct any words you have spelled incorrectly.

1. _____

2. _____

3. _____

4. _____

5. _____

6. _____

7. _____

8. _____

9. _____

10. _____

11. _____

12. _____

13. _____

14. _____

15. _____

16. _____

17. _____

18. _____

19. _____

20. _____

21. _____

22. _____

23. _____

24. _____

25. _____

Using Your Words:

Fill in the blanks with words from your spelling list.

1. Lisa_____ helped Julie braid her hair.

2. Jack's new puppy _____ wagged its tail for a treat.

3. His_____ action helped stop the car before it hit the crowd.

4. While we were on vacation, we took _____ of the pool and hot tub at the hotel.

5. The FedEx driver dropped off the _____ yesterday.

6. My aunt and uncle used an _____ in China to get their new son.

7. The _____ of the earthquake are horrifying.

8. How many _____ were taken in the bank robbery?

Day 87

As you hear them, write the spelling words for the day in the space provided. Be sure that you correct any words you have spelled incorrectly.

1. _____

2. _____

3. _____

4. _____

5. _____

6. _____

7. _____

8. _____

9. _____

10. _____

11. _____

12. _____

13. _____

14. _____

15. _____

16. _____

17. _____

18. _____

19. _____

20. _____

21. _____

22. _____

23. _____

24. _____

25. _____

Using Your Words:

Choose seven of today's spelling words and use them in a poem, short paragraph or silly story.

1._____

_____

2._____

_____

3._____

_____

4._____

_____

5._____

_____

6._____

_____

7._____

_____

Day 88

As you hear them, write the spelling words for the day in the space provided. Be sure that you correct any words you have spelled incorrectly.

1. _____

2. _____

3. _____

4. _____

5. _____

6. _____

7. _____

8. _____

9. _____

10. _____

11. _____

12. _____

13. _____

14. _____

15. _____

16. _____

17. _____

18. _____

19. _____

20. _____

21. _____

22. _____

23. _____

24. _____

25. _____

Using Your Words:

Unscramble these:

1. gatreos _____

2. naignmag _____

3. mrlaulyfh _____

4. eocanturmgeen _____

5. ggrabea _____

6. gmereayl _____

7. evgnauaaodst _____

8. ieasvlglr _____

9. ikcnapgag _____

10. nsgguelaa _____

Day 89

As you hear them, write the spelling words for the day in the space provided. Be sure that you correct any words you have spelled incorrectly.

1. _____

2. _____

3. _____

4. _____

5. _____

6. _____

7. _____

8. _____

9. _____

10. _____

11. _____

12. _____

13. _____

14. _____

15. _____

16. _____

17. _____

18. _____

19. _____

20. _____

21. _____

22. _____

23. _____

24. _____

25. _____

Using Your Words:

List as many words as you can which have the following letters (in order) in them.

udge

_____

_____

_____

_____

_____

_____

_____

_____

_____

_____

_____

Day 90

Spelling Lesson:

As you hear them, write the spelling words for the day in the space provided. Be sure that you correct any words you have spelled incorrectly.

1. _____

2. _____

3. _____

4. _____

5. _____

6. _____

7. _____

8. _____

9. _____

10. _____

11. _____

12. _____

13. _____

14. _____

15. _____

16. _____

17. _____

18. _____

19. _____

20. _____

21. _____

22. _____

23. _____

24. _____

25. _____

Using Your Words:

Make a rhyme or silly story using seven of today's spelling words.

_____

_____

_____

_____

_____

_____

_____

_____

_____

_____

Day 91

As you hear them, write the spelling words for the day in the space provided. Be sure that you correct any words you have spelled incorrectly.

1. _____

2. _____

3. _____

4. _____

5. _____

6. _____

7. _____

8. _____

9. _____

10. _____

11. _____

12. _____

13. _____

14. _____

15. _____

16. _____

17. _____

18. _____

19. _____

20. _____

21. _____

22. _____

23. _____

24. _____

25. _____

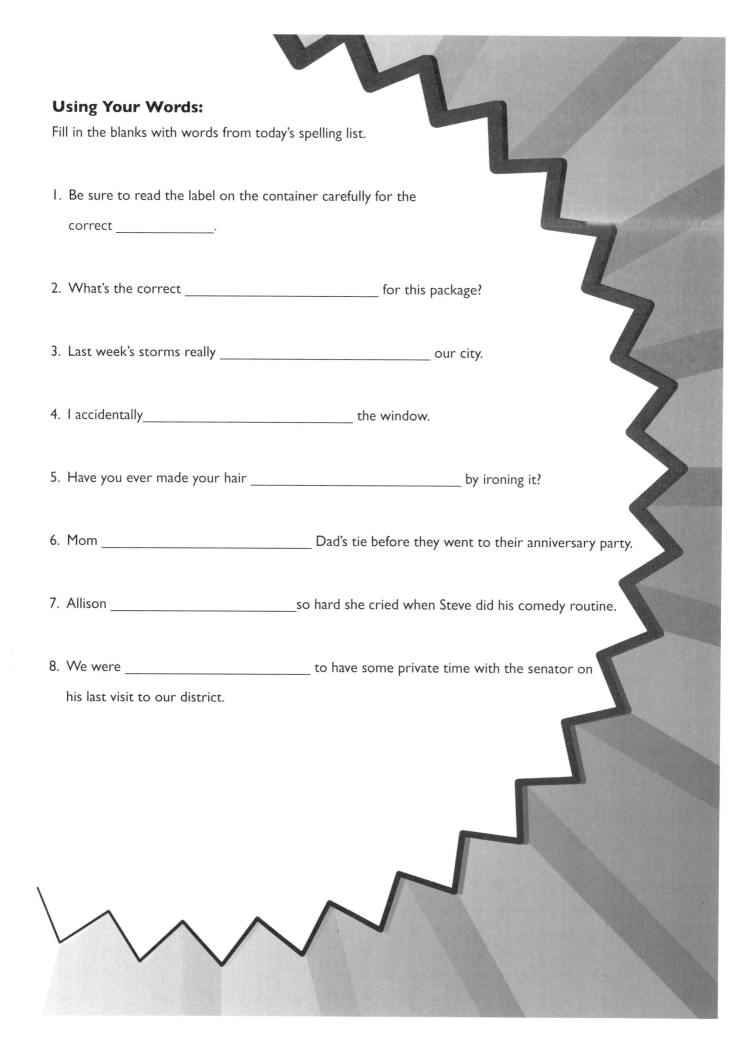

Using Your Words:

Fill in the blanks with words from today's spelling list.

1. Be sure to read the label on the container carefully for the

    correct _____.

2. What's the correct _____ for this package?

3. Last week's storms really _____ our city.

4. I accidentally_____ the window.

5. Have you ever made your hair _____ by ironing it?

6. Mom _____ Dad's tie before they went to their anniversary party.

7. Allison _____so hard she cried when Steve did his comedy routine.

8. We were _____ to have some private time with the senator on

    his last visit to our district.

Day 92

Spelling Lesson:

As you hear them, write the spelling words for the day in the space provided. Be sure that you correct any words you have spelled incorrectly.

1. _____

2. _____

3. _____

4. _____

5. _____

6. _____

7. _____

8. _____

9. _____

10. _____

11. _____

12. _____

13. _____

14. _____

15. _____

16. _____

17. _____

18. _____

19. _____

20. _____

21. _____

22. _____

23. _____

24. _____

25. _____

Using Your Words

Can you find the Words?

```
Y  S  C  G  B  W  Q  J  M  B  D  X  G  G  E
H  Y  A  F  N  K  I  I  X  A  M  N  V  G  G
D  C  X  C  U  I  D  D  U  Y  I  U  E  P  A
P  X  D  C  R  G  G  G  N  T  L  A  B  T
J  V  M  C  E  I  H  D  E  E  L  N  T  U  T
X  M  Q  T  U  T  L  T  U  O  T  B  N  D  A
D  Q  S  Q  E  U  H  E  C  R  O  S  W  G  W
P  Y  G  R  K  G  G  P  G  T  G  V  N  E  N
Z  J  S  M  I  E  Z  A  A  E  H  S  U  T  N
Z  X  K  A  P  R  I  V  I  L  E  G  E  I  A
F  K  R  G  N  I  G  D  U  M  S  Q  R  N  U
K  T  Y  X  B  U  D  G  I  N  G  K  X  G  G
S  T  W  E  G  A  V  A  R  L  C  L  H  X  H
U  J  S  L  C  B  Y  X  K  E  T  I  U  H  T
V  Z  N  J  Z  S  A  C  O  T  S  V  G  L  Y
```

Words Used

budgeting

budging

college

daughters

grudging

midgets

naughty

privilege

ravage

sacrilege

smudging

straightening

wattage

widgets

Spelling Lesson:

As you hear them, write the spelling words for the day in the space provided. Be sure that you correct any words you have spelled incorrectly.

1. _____

2. _____

3. _____

4. _____

5. _____

6. _____

7. _____

8. _____

9. _____

10. _____

11. _____

12. _____

13. _____

14. _____

15. _____

16. _____

17. _____

18. _____

19. _____

20. _____

21. _____

22. _____

23. _____

24. _____

25. _____

Using Your Words:

Use a dictionary to find the definitions of these spelling words. Then, use them in a sentence.

1. evade _____

_____

2. invade _____

_____

3. persuade _____

_____

4. spade _____

_____

5. enable _____

_____

6. gable _____

_____

7. wade _____

_____

8. ruble _____

_____

9. feeble _____

_____

10. abrade _____

_____

Day 94

Spelling Lesson:

As you hear them, write the spelling words for the day in the space provided. Be sure that you correct any words you have spelled incorrectly.

1. _____

2. _____

3. _____

4. _____

5. _____

6. _____

7. _____

8. _____

9. _____

10. _____

11. _____

12. _____

13. _____

14. _____

15. _____

16. _____

17. _____

18. _____

19. _____

20. _____

21. _____

22. _____

23. _____

24. _____

25. _____

Using Your Words:

Fill in the blanks with words from your spelling list.

1. Jack needs to _____ 140 pounds to wrestle at the welterweight level.

2. When we took a trip to Maine this winter, we had a _____ ride.

3. My _____, Mrs. Reed, makes wonderful chocolate chip cookies.

4. The bald _____ is a very graceful bird.

5. We met Emily and Scott for _____ yesterday.

6. At its _____, the population of our city was 150,000.

7. Her voice was so quiet, we edged closer to the front so that we could

   hear her _____.

8. Those old floorboards in the attic really _____!

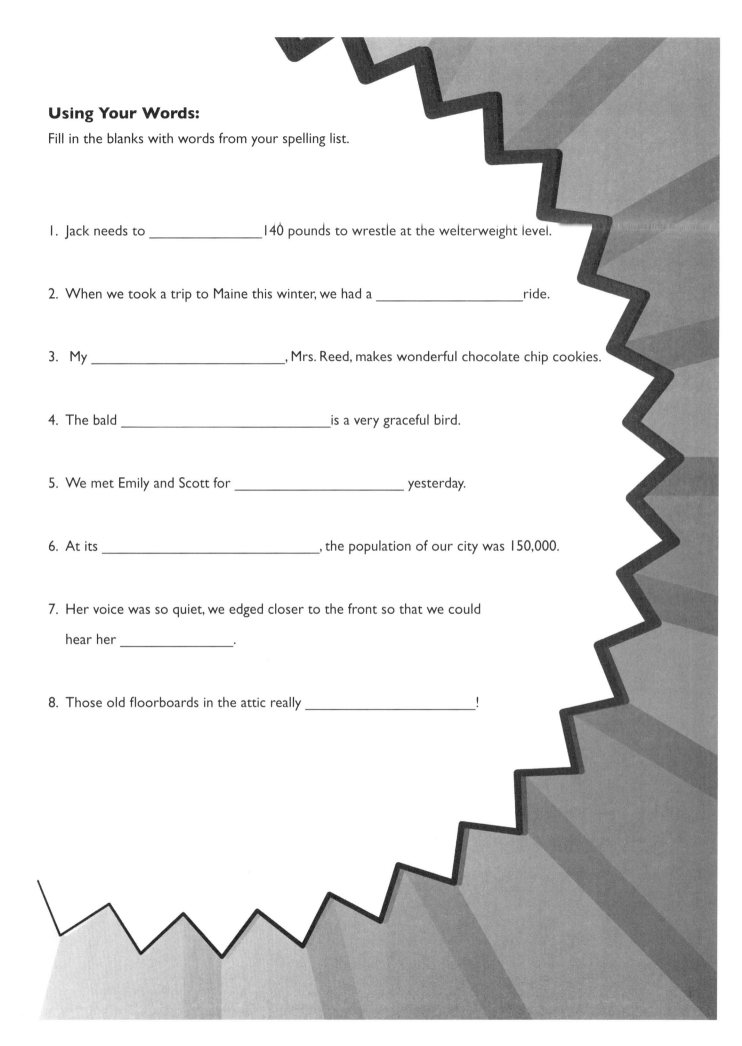

Day 95

As you hear them, write the spelling words for the day in the space provided. Be sure that you correct any words you have spelled incorrectly.

1. _____

2. _____

3. _____

4. _____

5. _____

6. _____

7. _____

8. _____

9. _____

10. _____

11. _____

12. _____

13. _____

14. _____

15. _____

16. _____

17. _____

18. _____

19. _____

20. _____

21. _____

22. _____

23. _____

24. _____

25. _____

Using Your Words:

List as many words as you can which have the following letters (in order) in them.

eak

_____

_____

_____

_____

_____

_____

_____

_____

_____

Day 96

Spelling Lesson:

As you hear them, write the spelling words for the day in the space provided. Be sure that you correct any words you have spelled incorrectly.

1. _____

2. _____

3. _____

4. _____

5. _____

6. _____

7. _____

8. _____

9. _____

10. _____

11. _____

12. _____

13. _____

14. _____

15. _____

16. _____

17. _____

18. _____

19. _____

20. _____

21. _____

22. _____

23. _____

24. _____

25. _____

Using Your Words:

Unscramble these:

1. hdweige   _____

2. ledhegis   _____

3. eednwkae   _____

4. ksqauey   _____

5. naeedsk   _____

6. ckraede   _____

7. eodoibhnhogr   _____

8. kwdeotao   _____

9. ekfra   _____

10. ponesk   _____

Spelling Lesson:

As you hear them, write the spelling words for the day in the space provided. Be sure that you correct any words you have spelled incorrectly.

1. _____

2. _____

3. _____

4. _____

5. _____

6. _____

7. _____

8. _____

9. _____

10. _____

11. _____

12. _____

13. _____

14. _____

15. _____

16. _____

17. _____

18. _____

19. _____

20. _____

21. _____

22. _____

23. _____

24. _____

25. _____

Using your words:

Make a rhyme or silly story using seven of today's spelling words.

_____

_____

_____

_____

_____

_____

_____

_____

_____

_____

Day 98

As you hear them, write the spelling words for the day in the space provided. Be sure that you correct any words you have spelled incorrectly.

1. _____

2. _____

3. _____

4. _____

5. _____

6. _____

7. _____

8. _____

9. _____

10. _____

11. _____

12. _____

13. _____

14. _____

15. _____

16. _____

17. _____

18. _____

19. _____

20. _____

21. _____

22. _____

23. _____

24. _____

25. _____

Using Your Words:

Make as many words
as you can from the
following word:

overhaul

Day 99

As you hear them, write the spelling words for the day in the space provided. Be sure that you correct any words you have spelled incorrectly.

1. _____

2. _____

3. _____

4. _____

5. _____

6. _____

7. _____

8. _____

9. _____

10. _____

11. _____

12. _____

13. _____

14. _____

15. _____

16. _____

17. _____

18. _____

19. _____

20. _____

21. _____

22. _____

23. _____

24. _____

25. _____

Using Your Words:

Use a dictionary to find the definitions of these words. Then, use each of them in a sentence.

1. rebel (1)_____

_____

2. rebel (2)_____

_____

3. repel_____

_____

4. caul_____

_____

5. caterwaul_____

_____

6. compel_____

_____

7. repulse_____

_____

8. dispel_____

_____

Day 100

As you hear them, write the spelling words for the day in the space provided. Be sure that you correct any words you have spelled incorrectly.

1. _____

2. _____

3. _____

4. _____

5. _____

6. _____

7. _____

8. _____

9. _____

10. _____

11. _____

12. _____

13. _____

14. _____

15. _____

16. _____

17. _____

18. _____

19. _____

20. _____

21. _____

22. _____

23. _____

24. _____

25. _____

Using Your Words

Can you find the Words?

```
C  F  U  V  K  Y  A  H  A  G  D  D  X  R  D
C  U  D  D  M  H  R  K  J  E  Z  E  W  N  E
H  O  B  E  C  A  G  X  S  H  Q  L  U  A  L
R  E  W  O  L  F  I  L  U  A  C  U  U  R  L
V  D  X  T  Y  U  U  Y  T  U  E  A  Q  E  E
Q  S  E  C  J  P  A  U  P  V  S  H  R  B  P
A  V  Q  K  E  Q  N  W  I  O  C  R  K  E  E
U  Z  G  R  E  L  B  S  R  X  W  E  G  L  R
H  P  Q  I  U  I  L  B  T  E  Z  V  L  L  Q
X  J  B  W  D  U  R  E  A  H  T  O  Z  I  R
W  Q  K  E  P  J  B  H  N  L  K  A  A  O  K
O  T  B  M  L  Q  M  G  S  T  V  M  C  N  W
K  U  O  V  T  S  P  O  O  K  I  E  S  T  N
K  C  D  E  L  L  E  P  M  O  C  D  H  R  W
F  Z  Y  H  Q  Y  F  A  U  L  T  E  D  O  H
```

Words Used

caterwauled

cauliflower

compelled

compulsive

excellent

faulted

overhauled

rebellion

repelled

repulsed

shrieked

spookiest

Day 101

As you hear them, write the spelling words for the day in the space provided. Be sure that you correct any words you have spelled incorrectly.

1. _____

2. _____

3. _____

4. _____

5. _____

6. _____

7. _____

8. _____

9. _____

10. _____

11. _____

12. _____

13. _____

14. _____

15. _____

16. _____

17. _____

18. _____

19. _____

20. _____

21. _____

22. _____

23. _____

24. _____

25. _____

Using Your Words:

List as many words as you can which have the following letters (in order) in them.

auled

_____

_____

_____

_____

_____

_____

_____

_____

_____

_____

Day 102

As you hear them, write the spelling words for the day in the space provided. Be sure that you correct any words you have spelled incorrectly.

1. _____

2. _____

3. _____

4. _____

5. _____

6. _____

7. _____

8. _____

9. _____

10. _____

11. _____

12. _____

13. _____

14. _____

15. _____

16. _____

17. _____

18. _____

19. _____

20. _____

21. _____

22. _____

23. _____

24. _____

25. _____

Using Your Words:

Fill in the blanks with words from today's spelling list.

1. _____ and his parents stayed at a _____

   when they visited their relatives in San Diego.

2. The _____ on the soup can says that there are 100 grams of

   sodium in the soup.

3. We will need to _____ our dinner plans with_____.

4. I am hoping to study abroad in _____ next year.

5. Kristin was an _____ to pick me up after school.

6. In the winter, I really like sleeping in my _____ pajamas.

7. The atomic symbol for_____ is Ni.

8. My mother was asked to be a _____ in the Historical

   Society's fashion show.

Spelling Lesson:

As you hear them, write the spelling words for the day in the space provided. Be sure that you correct any words you have spelled incorrectly.

1. _____

2. _____

3. _____

4. _____

5. _____

6. _____

7. _____

8. _____

9. _____

10. _____

11. _____

12. _____

13. _____

14. _____

15. _____

16. _____

17. _____

18. _____

19. _____

20. _____

21. _____

22. _____

23. _____

24. _____

25. _____

Using Your Words

Make as many words as you can with the following letters (in order) in them:

els

_____

_____

_____

_____

_____

_____

_____

_____

_____

_____

Spelling Lesson:

As you hear them, write the spelling words for the day in the space provided. Be sure that you correct any words you have spelled incorrectly.

1. _____

2. _____

3. _____

4. _____

5. _____

6. _____

7. _____

8. _____

9. _____

10. _____

11. _____

12. _____

13. _____

14. _____

15. _____

16. _____

17. _____

18. _____

19. _____

20. _____

21. _____

22. _____

23. _____

24. _____

25. _____

Using Your Words:

Choose at least seven words from your spelling list and use them in a rhyme, silly story or sentences.

_____

_____

_____

_____

_____

_____

_____

_____

_____

_____

Spelling Lesson:

As you hear them, write the spelling words for the day in the space provided. Be sure that you correct any words you have spelled incorrectly.

1. _____

2. _____

3. _____

4. _____

5. _____

6. _____

7. _____

8. _____

9. _____

10. _____

11. _____

12. _____

13. _____

14. _____

15. _____

16. _____

17. _____

18. _____

19. _____

20. _____

21. _____

22. _____

23. _____

24. _____

25. _____

Using Your Words:

Sounds alike words:

Find the definitions of each of these words and then use them in a sentence.

counsel/council

1. _____

_____

2. _____

_____

Day 106

As you hear them, write the spelling words for the day in the space provided. Be sure that you correct any words you have spelled incorrectly.

1. _____

2. _____

3. _____

4. _____

5. _____

6. _____

7. _____

8. _____

9. _____

10. _____

11. _____

12. _____

13. _____

14. _____

15. _____

16. _____

17. _____

18. _____

19. _____

20. _____

21. _____

22. _____

23. _____

24. _____

25. _____

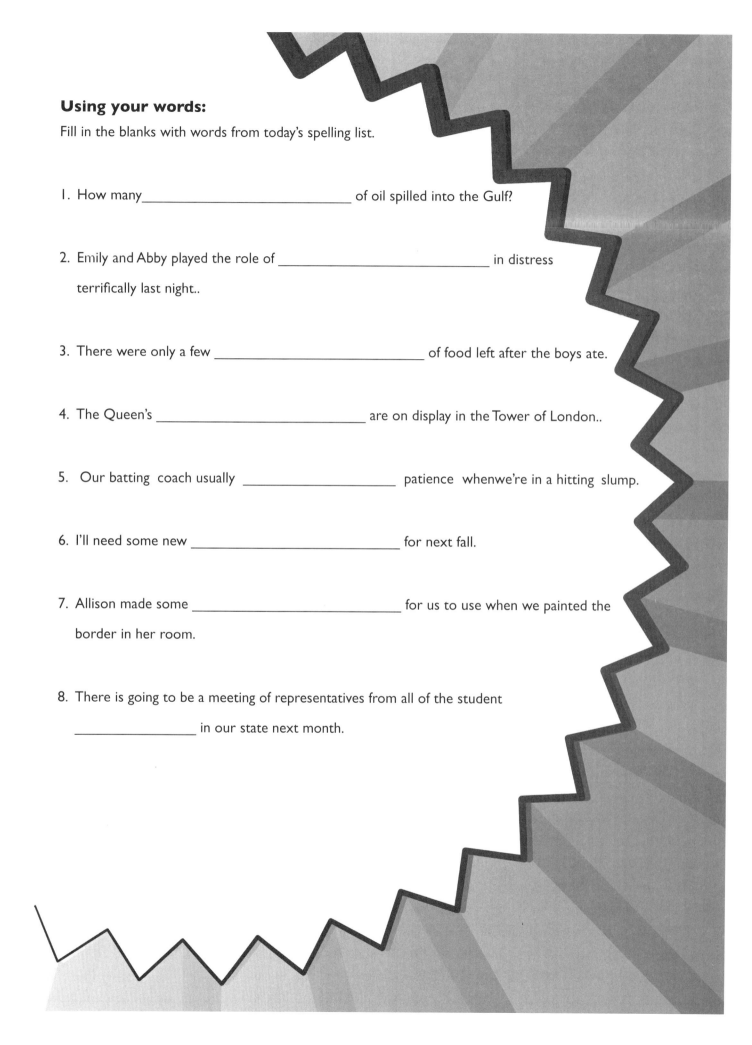

Using your words:

Fill in the blanks with words from today's spelling list.

1. How many _____ of oil spilled into the Gulf?

2. Emily and Abby played the role of _____ in distress

    terrifically last night..

3. There were only a few _____ of food left after the boys ate.

4. The Queen's _____ are on display in the Tower of London..

5. Our batting coach usually _____ patience whenwe're in a hitting slump.

6. I'll need some new _____ for next fall.

7. Allison made some _____ for us to use when we painted the

    border in her room.

8. There is going to be a meeting of representatives from all of the student

    _____ in our state next month.

Day 107

As you hear them, write the spelling words for the day in the space provided. Be sure that you correct any words you have spelled incorrectly.

1. _____

2. _____

3. _____

4. _____

5. _____

6. _____

7. _____

8. _____

9. _____

10. _____

11. _____

12. _____

13. _____

14. _____

15. _____

16. _____

17. _____

18. _____

19. _____

20. _____

21. _____

22. _____

23. _____

24. _____

25. _____

Using Your Words:

Make as many words
as you can from the
following word:

marvelous

_____

_____

_____

_____

_____

_____

_____

_____

_____

_____

Spelling Lesson:

As you hear them, write the spelling words for the day in the space provided. Be sure that you correct any words you have spelled incorrectly.

1. _____   14. _____

2. _____   15. _____

3. _____   16. _____

4. _____   17. _____

5. _____   18. _____

6. _____   19. _____

7. _____   20. _____

8. _____   21. _____

9. _____   22. _____

10. _____   23. _____

11. _____   24. _____

12. _____   25. _____

13. _____

Using your words

Can You  **the Words?**

```
M K B Q D S B C T R Q I X M H
A A H L L M G U O O L C F D E
G G R I E F N L A L D O J W K
V N G V V N I P X E O U E F E
J I I O E C R V C S S N W R Q
V F X L N L J E O N L S E U E
R H I U E O O W K U I E L L C
O N O J W R E U F O P L R K I
G C N P L A R R S C U I Y D X
C I T W S M W A H L P N X L X
X S L E S S A T B I Y G P M C
F W L D C H I S E L I N G E D
W S U C S D F O Q Y L B T Y U
P S O T J S N I A L P A H C M
D N U L Y J S M O P B N N Q L
```

Words Used

barreling

chaplains

chiseling

colonel

councilor

counseling

counselor

jewelry

kernel

marvelously

pupils

tassels

tunneling

vigils

weasels

Day 109

As you hear them, write the spelling words for the day in the space provided. Be sure that you correct any words you have spelled incorrectly.

1. _____

2. _____

3. _____

4. _____

5. _____

6. _____

7. _____

8. _____

9. _____

10. _____

11. _____

12. _____

13. _____

14. _____

15. _____

16. _____

17. _____

18. _____

19. _____

20. _____

21. _____

22. _____

23. _____

24. _____

25. _____

Using Your Words:

Sound alike words:

Use a dictionary to find the meanings of the words you don't know; then use each of them correctly in a sentence.

fowl/foul
bowl/boll
duel/dual

1._____

_____

2._____

_____

3._____

_____

4._____

_____

5._____

_____

6._____

_____

Day 110

Spelling Lesson:

As you hear them, write the spelling words for the day in the space provided. Be sure that you correct any words you have spelled incorrectly.

1. _____

2. _____

3. _____

4. _____

5. _____

6. _____

7. _____

8. _____

9. _____

10. _____

11. _____

12. _____

13. _____

14. _____

15. _____

16. _____

17. _____

18. _____

19. _____

20. _____

21. _____

22. _____

23. _____

24. _____

25. _____

Using Your Words:

List as many words as you can with the following letters (in order) in them.

ilized

_____

_____

_____

_____

_____

_____

_____

_____

_____

_____

Spelling Lesson:

As you hear them, write the spelling words for the day in the space provided. Be sure that you correct any words you have spelled incorrectly.

1. _____

2. _____

3. _____

4. _____

5. _____

6. _____

7. _____

8. _____

9. _____

10. _____

11. _____

12. _____

13. _____

14. _____

15. _____

16. _____

17. _____

18. _____

19. _____

20. _____

21. _____

22. _____

23. _____

24. _____

25. _____

Using Your Words:

Unscramble these:

1. eoripus   _____

2. dbeevdile   _____

3. imelpreidq   _____

4. oniltsq   _____

5. anocvilziitiq   _____

6. lewcdosq   _____

7. augsrq   _____

8. elrueefd   _____

9. ldedeu   _____

10. rueltcy   _____

Day 112

Spelling Lesson:

As you hear them, write the spelling words for the day in the space provided. Be sure that you correct any words you have spelled incorrectly.

1. _____

2. _____

3. _____

4. _____

5. _____

6. _____

7. _____

8. _____

9. _____

10. _____

11. _____

12. _____

13. _____

14. _____

15. _____

16. _____

17. _____

18. _____

19. _____

20. _____

21. _____

22. _____

23. _____

24. _____

25. _____

Using Your Words:

Choose at least seven words from your spelling list and use each in a rhyme, poem, paragraph or silly story.

1._____

_____

2._____

_____

3._____

_____

4._____

_____

5._____

_____

6._____

_____

7._____

_____

Spelling Lesson:

As you hear them, write the spelling words for the day in the space provided. Be sure that you correct any words you have spelled incorrectly.

1. _____

2. _____

3. _____

4. _____

5. _____

6. _____

7. _____

8. _____

9. _____

10. _____

11. _____

12. _____

13. _____

14. _____

15. _____

16. _____

17. _____

18. _____

19. _____

20. _____

21. _____

22. _____

23. _____

24. _____

25. _____

Using Your Words:

List as many words as you can with the following letters (in order) in them.

ield

_____

_____

_____

_____

_____

_____

_____

_____

_____

_____

Day 114

Spelling Lesson:

As you hear them, write the spelling words for the day in the space provided. Be sure that you correct any words you have spelled incorrectly.

1. _____

2. _____

3. _____

4. _____

5. _____

6. _____

7. _____

8. _____

9. _____

10. _____

11. _____

12. _____

13. _____

14. _____

15. _____

16. _____

17. _____

18. _____

19. _____

20. _____

21. _____

22. _____

23. _____

24. _____

25. _____

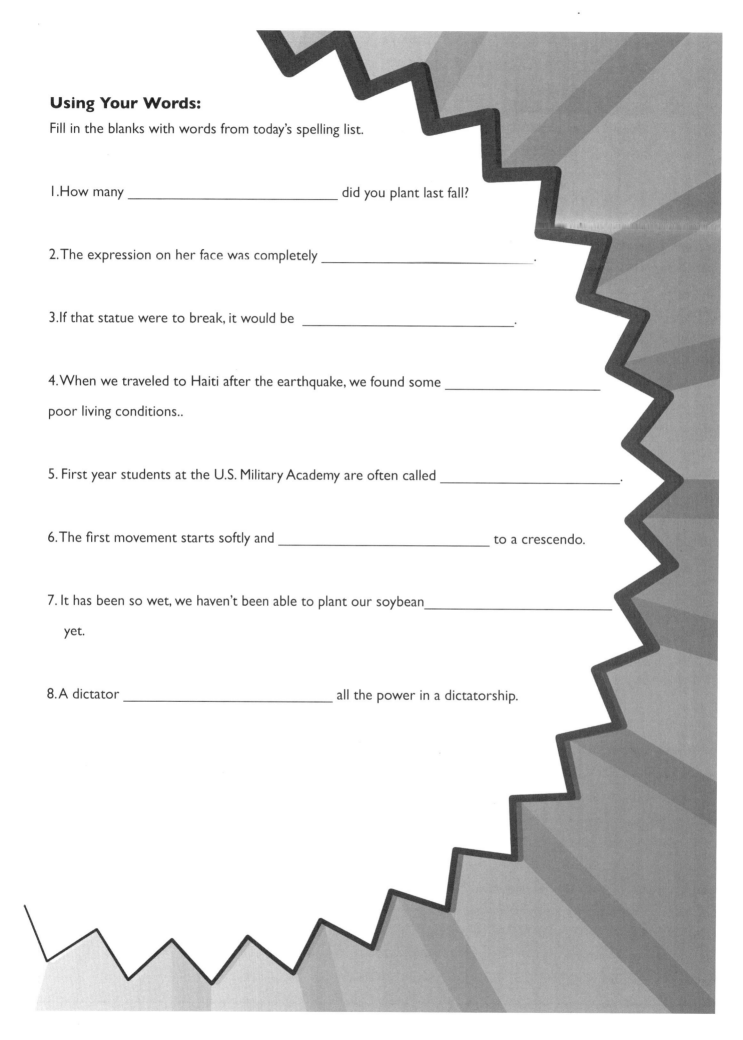

Using Your Words:

Fill in the blanks with words from today's spelling list.

1. How many _____ did you plant last fall?

2. The expression on her face was completely _____.

3. If that statue were to break, it would be _____.

4. When we traveled to Haiti after the earthquake, we found some _____ poor living conditions..

5. First year students at the U.S. Military Academy are often called _____.

6. The first movement starts softly and _____ to a crescendo.

7. It has been so wet, we haven't been able to plant our soybean_____ yet.

8. A dictator _____ all the power in a dictatorship.

Day 115

As you hear them, write the spelling words for the day in the space provided. Be sure that you correct any words you have spelled incorrectly.

1. _____

2. _____

3. _____

4. _____

5. _____

6. _____

7. _____

8. _____

9. _____

10. _____

11. _____

12. _____

13. _____

14. _____

15. _____

16. _____

17. _____

18. _____

19. _____

20. _____

21. _____

22. _____

23. _____

24. _____

25. _____

Using Your Words:

Unscramble these:

1. mabneaglea _____

2. beytriiaald _____

3. aralegbee _____

4. ltiub _____

5. ugitl _____

6. iedelwd _____

7. erbilud _____

8. esiddlhe _____

9. bibylripato _____

10. rfletiuoed _____

Spelling Lesson:

As you hear them, write the spelling words for the day in the space provided. Be sure that you correct any words you have spelled incorrectly.

1. _____   14. _____

2. _____   15. _____

3. _____   16. _____

4. _____   17. _____

5. _____   18. _____

6. _____   19. _____

7. _____   20. _____

8. _____   21. _____

9. _____   22. _____

10. _____   23. _____

11. _____   24. _____

12. _____   25. _____

13. _____

Using Your Words:

Can You find the Words?

```
Z Q E N K V S A W Z X R S G A
O U T F I E L D E R S E G E B
T C X X S C Z H U Q I Y N L I
B X H P N C Q W T T A I I B L
E M G A G A A P I G C E D A I
P J V N N V L R P B L L E T
W M L J I G I E D V M D E G I
G Y I K K B E D Q I V I I D E
J D A H A A U A L H N N F E S
W T R B B R H C B I S G Y L D
Q P O L P H Y Q W L U Q T W Q
R R Y G N I D L I G E B L O S
P G N I D L E I H S K P I N I
L N O U T F I E L D P P U K A
W L J X X N Y E I G C S G A L
```

Words Used

abilities

agreeably

building

changeable

cubing

fielding

gilding

guilty

knowledgeable

outfield

outfielders

probabilities

scalding

shielding

yielding

Spelling Lesson:

As you hear them, write the spelling words for the day in the space provided. Be sure that you correct any words you have spelled incorrectly.

1. _____

2. _____

3. _____

4. _____

5. _____

6. _____

7. _____

8. _____

9. _____

10. _____

11. _____

12. _____

13. _____

14. _____

15. _____

16. _____

17. _____

18. _____

19. _____

20. _____

21. _____

22. _____

23. _____

24. _____

25. _____

Using Your Words:

Use a dictionary to find the definitions of these spelling words. Then, use them correctly in a sentence.

1. indefatigable _____

_____

2. navigable _____

_____

3. society _____

_____

4. social _____

_____

5. liable _____

_____

6. reliable _____

_____

Day 118

Spelling Lesson:

As you hear them, write the spelling words for the day in the space provided. Be sure that you correct any words you have spelled incorrectly.

1. _____

2. _____

3. _____

4. _____

5. _____

6. _____

7. _____

8. _____

9. _____

10. _____

11. _____

12. _____

13. _____

14. _____

15. _____

16. _____

17. _____

18. _____

19. _____

20. _____

21. _____

22. _____

23. _____

24. _____

25. _____

Using Your Words:

Make as many words as
you can from the
following word

companionable

_____

_____

_____

_____

_____

_____

_____

_____

_____

Day 119

Spelling Lesson:

As you hear them, write the spelling words for the day in the space provided. Be sure that you correct any words you have spelled incorrectly.

1. _____

2. _____

3. _____

4. _____

5. _____

6. _____

7. _____

8. _____

9. _____

10. _____

11. _____

12. _____

13. _____

14. _____

15. _____

16. _____

17. _____

18. _____

19. _____

20. _____

21. _____

22. _____

23. _____

24. _____

25. _____

Using Your Words:

Unscramble these:

1. feureailnsbf _____

2. relsetayap _____

3. acmrobelpa _____

4. aseeodnlircb _____

5. rbilacevees _____

6. neferlouneabc _____

7. tipsibeiclaa _____

8. snilceaebap _____

9. bblaraee _____

10. belynasoaunr _____

Spelling Lesson:

As you hear them, write the spelling words for the day in the space provided. Be sure that you correct any words you have spelled incorrectly.

1. _____

2. _____

3. _____

4. _____

5. _____

6. _____

7. _____

8. _____

9. _____

10. _____

11. _____

12. _____

13. _____

14. _____

15. _____

16. _____

17. _____

18. _____

19. _____

20. _____

21. _____

22. _____

23. _____

24. _____

25. _____

Using Your Words:

Choose at least seven words from your spelling list and use them in a poem, rhyme, paragraph or silly story.

Evaluation Test #3

Fill in the blanks with the missing letters.

1. Do you like standing in a rec_____ line?

2. Most people enjoy going to a wedding rec _____.

3. I like people who are ch_____.

4. They did what they were asked to do ch_____.

5. It's no fun losing your l_____ on vacation.

6. Sometimes it's necessary to have a strict b_____.

7. When was post_____ less than a dime?

8. Cattle are sl _____ everyday in stockyards.

9. My neighbor enjoys lifting w _____.

10. The squ_____ wheel gets the grease.

11. Our motor needs to be overh_____.

12. The two reb_____ were caught and tried for treason.

13. Not all reb_____ are successful.

14. Some people are very imp_____.

15. I dislike people who are always qu_____.

16. People should act civ_____.

17. The pr_____ were caught by the police.

18. The outf_____ collided going for the fly ball.

19. They prob_____. didn't hear each other yell, "It's mine."

20. The mayor was unav_____ for comment.

Spelling Lesson:

As you hear them, write the spelling words for the day in the space provided. Be sure that you correct any words you have spelled incorrectly.

1. _____

2. _____

3. _____

4. _____

5. _____

6. _____

7. _____

8. _____

9. _____

10. _____

11. _____

12. _____

13. _____

14. _____

15. _____

16. _____

17. _____

18. _____

19. _____

20. _____

21. _____

22. _____

23. _____

24. _____

25. _____

Using Your Words:

Fill in the blanks with words from today's spelling list.

1. During World War II, _____ gardens were

   sometimes called 'Victory gardens.

2. The weather in the south in the spring is sometimes very _____.

3. If you're traveling to another country, a good guidebookis an _____

   travel companion..

4. While he didn't win the race, he did finish in a _____ amount of time.

5. Last winter, after the snowstorm, the roads in the mountains were _____

   for several weeks.

6. Some products, like _____ diapers, are not environmentally

   friendly.

7. Mark's actions toward Josh were_____.

8. Even on weekends, my parents were _____ up by six am.

Day 122

Spelling Lesson:

As you hear them, write the spelling words for the day in the space provided. Be sure that you correct any words you have spelled incorrectly.

1. _____

2. _____

3. _____

4. _____

5. _____

6. _____

7. _____

8. _____

9. _____

10. _____

11. _____

12. _____

13. _____

14. _____

15. _____

16. _____

17. _____

18. _____

19. _____

20. _____

21. _____

22. _____

23. _____

24. _____

25. _____

Using Your Words:

Make as many words as you
can with the letters from
the following word:

inhospitable

_____

_____

_____

_____

_____

_____

_____

_____

_____

_____

Day 123

As you hear them, write the spelling words for the day in the space provided. Be sure that you correct any words you have spelled incorrectly.

1. _____

2. _____

3. _____

4. _____

5. _____

6. _____

7. _____

8. _____

9. _____

10. _____

11. _____

12. _____

13. _____

14. _____

15. _____

16. _____

17. _____

18. _____

19. _____

20. _____

21. _____

22. _____

23. _____

24. _____

25. _____

Using Your Words

Using a dictionary, find the definitions of these spelling words. Then, use each correctly in a sentence.

1. potable_____

_____

2. regrettable_____

_____

3. detestable_____

_____

4. irrefutable_____

_____

5. indisputable_____

_____

6. inscrutable_____

_____

Spelling Lesson:

As you hear them, write the spelling words for the day in the space provided. Be sure that you correct any words you have spelled incorrectly.

1. _____

2. _____

3. _____

4. _____

5. _____

6. _____

7. _____

8. _____

9. _____

10. _____

11. _____

12. _____

13. _____

14. _____

15. _____

16. _____

17. _____

18. _____

19. _____

20. _____

21. _____

22. _____

23. _____

24. _____

25. _____

Using your words:

Choose at least seven words from your spelling list and write a silly story or poem using them.

_____

_____

_____

_____

_____

_____

_____

_____

_____

_____

_____

Spelling Lesson:

As you hear them, write the spelling words for the day in the space provided. Be sure that you correct any words you have spelled incorrectly.

1. _____

2. _____

3. _____

4. _____

5. _____

6. _____

7. _____

8. _____

9. _____

10. _____

11. _____

12. _____

13. _____

14. _____

15. _____

16. _____

17. _____

18. _____

19. _____

20. _____

21. _____

22. _____

23. _____

24. _____

25. _____

Using Your Words:

List as many words as you can with the following letters (in order) in them:

ible

Day 126

Spelling Lesson:

As you hear them, write the spelling words for the day in the space provided. Be sure that you correct any words you have spelled incorrectly.

1. _____

2. _____

3. _____

4. _____

5. _____

6. _____

7. _____

8. _____

9. _____

10. _____

11. _____

12. _____

13. _____

14. _____

15. _____

16. _____

17. _____

18. _____

19. _____

20. _____

21. _____

22. _____

23. _____

24. _____

25. _____

Using Your Words:

Fill in the blanks with words from today's spelling list.

1. The new coat of paint made our fence look _____ again.

2. When the circus acrobat slipped, the audience gasped _____.

3. Jack and Steve went to play _____ tennis with Mark and Scott.

4. That new cell phone is _____ easy to use.

5. Our legislature passed a few laws that seem to be _____ and

   should be repealed.

6. It's always a good idea to sign your name _____.

7. During the Middle Ages, _____ were the ruling class.

8. How many _____ is a US dollar worth?

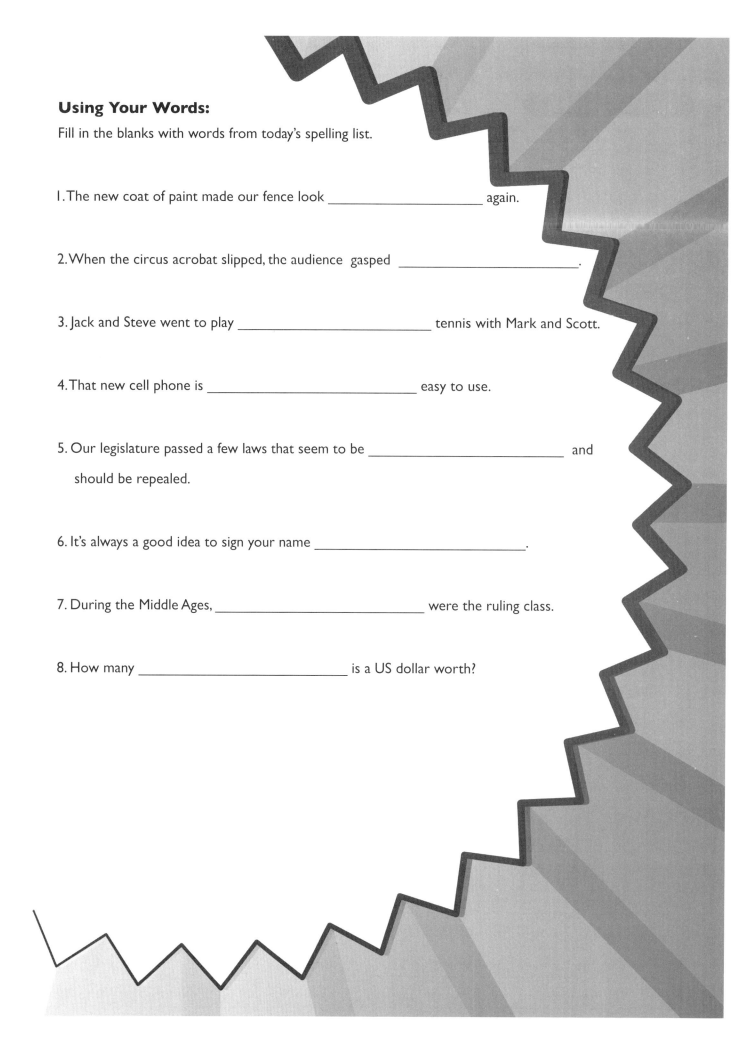

Spelling Lesson:

As you hear them, write the spelling words for the day in the space provided. Be sure that you correct any words you have spelled incorrectly.

1. _____

2. _____

3. _____

4. _____

5. _____

6. _____

7. _____

8. _____

9. _____

10. _____

11. _____

12. _____

13. _____

14. _____

15. _____

16. _____

17. _____

18. _____

19. _____

20. _____

21. _____

22. _____

23. _____

24. _____

25. _____

Using Your Words:

Unscramble these:

1. evsei   _____

2. rcriinilgtobiiy _____

3. gatnliby   _____

4. lignientlet   _____

5. iuealvlnab   _____

6. ebalub   _____

7. iytoilbn   _____

8. olbfie   _____

9. eduaiecn   _____

10. idanotiu   _____

Day 128

Spelling Lesson:

As you hear them, write the spelling words for the day in the space provided. Be sure that you correct any words you have spelled incorrectly.

1. _____

2. _____

3. _____

4. _____

5. _____

6. _____

7. _____

8. _____

9. _____

10. _____

11. _____

12. _____

13. _____

14. _____

15. _____

16. _____

17. _____

18. _____

19. _____

20. _____

21. _____

22. _____

23. _____

24. _____

25. _____

Using Your Words:

Can You  find the Words?

```
A   D   Y   V   S   Z   S   W   L   T   J   N   W   I   H
U   W   G   T   E   L   I   E   R   J   O   W   E   A   F
D   N   B   L   I   Z   E   O   L   M   F   K   H   R   Z
I   O   J   X   T   L   U   G   L   B   A   R   P   S   E
T   X   H   C   I   B   I   A   A   A   I   M   E   C   S
O   C   F   D   L   P   S   B   D   L   N   O   N   H   I
R   F   D   I   I   D   S   R   J   J   I   E   F   V   E
I   O   N   B   B   Q   D   A   Q   G   G   T   E   V   V
U   G   H   N   I   E   C   E   L   I   N   E   I   Q   E
M   B   W   D   S   G   E   Z   L   M   N   A   D   E   S
Z   Z   Q   W   S   A   O   L   Y   X   F   O   T   N   S
Q   U   U   H   O   J   E   S   Y   I   X   I   L   N   U
X   O   H   Y   P   T   L   Y   H   U   W   I   M   J   I
U   O   X   A   N   A   L   L   E   G   I   A   N   C   E
O   N   L   I   E   L   B   A   T   S   N   O   C   E   S
```

Words Used

allegiance

auditorium

constable

foibles

intangibility

intelligence

legalities

nephew

niece

possibilities

psalm

salmon

sieve

troubling

Day 129

Spelling Lesson:

As you hear them, write the spelling words for the day in the space provided. Be sure that you correct any words you have spelled incorrectly.

1. _____

2. _____

3. _____

4. _____

5. _____

6. _____

7. _____

8. _____

9. _____

10. _____

11. _____

12. _____

13. _____

14. _____

15. _____

16. _____

17. _____

18. _____

19. _____

20. _____

21. _____

22. _____

23. _____

24. _____

25. _____

Using Your Words:

Use a dictionary to find the definitions of these spelling words; then use each in a sentence.

1.fallible_____

_____

2. gullible_____

_____

3.discernible_____

_____

4.negligible_____

_____

5.comprehensible_____

_____

6. feasible_____

_____

Day 130

Spelling Lesson:

As you hear them, write the spelling words for the day in the space provided. Be sure that you correct any words you have spelled incorrectly.

1. _____

2. _____

3. _____

4. _____

5. _____

6. _____

7. _____

8. _____

9. _____

10. _____

11. _____

12. _____

13. _____

14. _____

15. _____

16. _____

17. _____

18. _____

19. _____

20. _____

21. _____

22. _____

23. _____

24. _____

25. _____

Using Your Words:

Make as many words as you can from the letters in the following word:

incomprehensibly

_____

_____

_____

_____

_____

_____

_____

_____

_____

_____

Spelling Lesson:

As you hear them, write the spelling words for the day in the space provided. Be sure that you correct any words you have spelled incorrectly.

1. _____

2. _____

3. _____

4. _____

5. _____

6. _____

7. _____

8. _____

9. _____

10. _____

11. _____

12. _____

13. _____

14. _____

15. _____

16. _____

17. _____

18. _____

19. _____

20. _____

21. _____

22. _____

23. _____

24. _____

25. _____

Using your words:

Contractions

Write the words which are combined to make the contraction shown.

1 It's _____

2. They're _____

3. There's _____

4. You're_____

5. We're_____

6. He's _____

7. She's _____

8. Here're_____ .

Sequential Spelling Level 4 - Student Workbook

Spelling Lesson:

As you hear them, write the spelling words for the day in the space provided. Be sure that you correct any words you have spelled incorrectly.

1. _____

2. _____

3. _____

4. _____

5. _____

6. _____

7. _____

8. _____

9. _____

10. _____

11. _____

12. _____

13. _____

14. _____

15. _____

16. _____

17. _____

18. _____

19. _____

20. _____

21. _____

22. _____

23. _____

24. _____

25. _____

Using Your Words

Can you  the words?

```
M  E  V  I  R  Y  D  J  C  C  L  Y  O  Z  E
U  Y  V  T  G  I  G  F  O  F  N  R  W  M  L
S  O  L  I  V  P  D  C  M  M  L  A  S  P  B
T  I  K  I  S  F  L  V  P  T  H  N  K  S  I
A  N  D  A  U  N  F  Q  R  O  N  O  Z  M  S
C  E  A  P  P  R  E  H  E  N  S  I  O  N  N
H  G  S  M  H  M  K  F  H  Z  R  S  X  Z  O
E  L  V  S  I  O  M  J  E  A  W  I  R  M  P
T  I  R  P  D  U  R  Q  N  D  R  V  A  Z  S
V  G  G  H  Q  S  B  R  S  Q  L  A  G  T  E
S  E  I  T  I  L  I  B  I  S  N  E  S  G  R
R  N  N  S  M  X  J  Z  V  F  T  Q  U  V  R
J  C  B  X  M  L  X  K  E  K  I  B  B  K  I
S  E  I  C  A  L  L  A  F  Z  O  E  E  F  M
N  T  E  R  R  I  F  I  E  D  P  A  D  D  K
```

Words Used

apprehension

comprehensive

debts

defensive

divide

fallacies

horrified

irresponsible

mustache

negligence

psalm

sensibilities

terrified

visionary

Day 133

As you hear them, write the spelling words for the day in the space provided. Be sure that you correct any words you have spelled incorrectly.

1. _____

2. _____

3. _____

4. _____

5. _____

6. _____

7. _____

8. _____

9. _____

10. _____

11. _____

12. _____

13. _____

14. _____

15. _____

16. _____

17. _____

18. _____

19. _____

20. _____

21. _____

22. _____

23. _____

24. _____

25. _____

Using Your Words:

List as many words as you can with the following letters (in order) in them.

bble

_____

_____

_____

_____

_____

_____

_____

_____

_____

Day 134

Spelling Lesson:

As you hear them, write the spelling words for the day in the space provided. Be sure that you correct any words you have spelled incorrectly.

1. _____

2. _____

3. _____

4. _____

5. _____

6. _____

7. _____

8. _____

9. _____

10. _____

11. _____

12. _____

13. _____

14. _____

15. _____

16. _____

17. _____

18. _____

19. _____

20. _____

21. _____

22. _____

23. _____

24. _____

25. _____

Using Your Words:

Fill in the blanks with words from today's spelling list.

1. How can we _____ thank you for all your help?

2. Allison seemed to have an _____ supply of energy as we worked refinishing the desk.

3. Emma got her learner's_____ yesterday.

4. It's very difficult to get along with someone as _____ as she is.

5. Dressed in camouflage, the soldier was almost _____ to the enemy.

6. Our attorney said that the evidence would be _____in court.

7. Sam drove one of the _____ in the homecoming parade.

8. Jody's pet fawn sometimes _____ the bushes.

Day 135

Spelling Lesson:

As you hear them, write the spelling words for the day in the space provided. Be sure that you correct any words you have spelled incorrectly.

1. _____

2. _____

3. _____

4. _____

5. _____

6. _____

7. _____

8. _____

9. _____

10. _____

11. _____

12. _____

13. _____

14. _____

15. _____

16. _____

17. _____

18. _____

19. _____

20. _____

21. _____

22. _____

23. _____

24. _____

25. _____

Using Your Words:

Unscramble these:

1. obistyspiil   _____

2. eeduc   _____

3. monpsrsiei   _____

4. tncpemtebloi   _____

5. oscetilbbum   _____

6. bbeladb   _____

7. fdeu   _____

8. edlqubib   _____

9. ticuniirsylidbett   _____

10. tipybilaisiu   _____

Day 136

Spelling Lesson:

As you hear them, write the spelling words for the day in the space provided. Be sure that you correct any words you have spelled incorrectly.

1. _____

2. _____

3. _____

4. _____

5. _____

6. _____

7. _____

8. _____

9. _____

10. _____

11. _____

12. _____

13. _____

14. _____

15. _____

16. _____

17. _____

18. _____

19. _____

20. _____

21. _____

22. _____

23. _____

24. _____

25. _____

Using your words:

Choose at least seven words from your spelling list and use them in a rhyme, poem, paragraph or silly story.

Spelling Lesson:

As you hear them, write the spelling words for the day in the space provided. Be sure that you correct any words you have spelled incorrectly.

1. _____   14. _____

2. _____   15. _____

3. _____   16. _____

4. _____   17. _____

5. _____   18. _____

6. _____   19. _____

7. _____   20. _____

8. _____   21. _____

9. _____   22. _____

10. _____   23. _____

11. _____   24. _____

12. _____   25. _____

13. _____

Using Your Words:

Fill in the blanks with words from today's spelling list.

1. Aunt Fran made really good peach _____ for dessert.

2. At the end of the day, I like to sink into a fragrant _____ bath.

3. Jim and Tim can sometimes be _____. It must be because they're twins!

4. Our baseball teams were both _____ today.

5. In my horseback riding class, I learned how to saddle and _____ my horse today.

6. Uncle Dan really likes to play _____. He's a good _____.

7. Jessica likes to _____ when she's waiting for the doctor.

8. If we _____ too long, we won't get home in time for supper.

Day 138

Spelling Lesson:

As you hear them, write the spelling words for the day in the space provided. Be sure that you correct any words you have spelled incorrectly.

1. _____   14. _____

2. _____   15. _____

3. _____   16. _____

4. _____   17. _____

5. _____   18. _____

6. _____   19. _____

7. _____   20. _____

8. _____   21. _____

9. _____   22. _____

10. _____   23. _____

11. _____   24. _____

12. _____   25. _____

13. _____

Using Your Words:

List as many words as you can that have the following letters (in order) in them.

oodle

_____

_____

_____

_____

_____

_____

_____

_____

_____

Spelling Lesson:

As you hear them, write the spelling words for the day in the space provided. Be sure that you correct any words you have spelled incorrectly.

1. _____

2. _____

3. _____

4. _____

5. _____

6. _____

7. _____

8. _____

9. _____

10. _____

11. _____

12. _____

13. _____

14. _____

15. _____

16. _____

17. _____

18. _____

19. _____

20. _____

21. _____

22. _____

23. _____

24. _____

25. _____

Using Your Words:

Unscramble these:

1. bbuldeb   _____

2. bebhldo   _____

3. cnsstoeobleb   _____

4. edelhwed   _____

5. lsddie   _____

6. leogdf   _____

7. irepldef   _____

8. daeddlw   _____

9. nodeol   _____

10. eweelddh   _____

Day 140

As you hear them, write the spelling words for the day in the space provided. Be sure that you correct any words you have spelled incorrectly.

1. _____

2. _____

3. _____

4. _____

5. _____

6. _____

7. _____

8. _____

9. _____

10. _____

11. _____

12. _____

13. _____

14. _____

15. _____

16. _____

17. _____

18. _____

19. _____

20. _____

21. _____

22. _____

23. _____

24. _____

25. _____

Using Your Words

Can you  the words?

```
U M E I V E X V D Z L D G P I
I K F E U D E D M B M A N M D
T R O U B L I N G R D W I G L
O U Q V A B G H Z I G D L N I
C G M B V V W X Q P G L D I N
A B M J S A G M H N Y I E F G
R Q M P J E Q O I R Y N E L U
I W Q E F O V R B T O G H O B
S E N O T S E L B B O C W G E
H E Q Y L F B J O L L U G Z D
Q G N I L D A R C W T I I B D
V B T I A D H U I J E L N I K
U M P Q O G T L U D O R S G W
S G T U A I W O O D A K E U N
R O B S K T R R I K C L C W M
```

Words Used

bridal

cobblestones

cradling

dawdling

feuded

gobbling

golfing

idling

idolize

pilfering

troubling

werewolves

wheedling

Day 141

As you hear them, write the spelling words for the day in the space provided. Be sure that you correct any words you have spelled incorrectly.

1. _____

2. _____

3. _____

4. _____

5. _____

6. _____

7. _____

8. _____

9. _____

10. _____

11. _____

12. _____

13. _____

14. _____

15. _____

16. _____

17. _____

18. _____

19. _____

20. _____

21. _____

22. _____

23. _____

24. _____

25. _____

Using your words:

Sound alike words:

Use each of these words in
a sentence correctly.

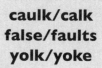

**caulk/calk
false/faults
yolk/yoke**

1._____

_____

2._____

_____

3._____

_____

4._____

_____

5._____

_____

6._____

_____

Spelling Lesson:

As you hear them, write the spelling words for the day in the space provided. Be sure that you correct any words you have spelled incorrectly.

1. _____

2. _____

3. _____

4. _____

5. _____

6. _____

7. _____

8. _____

9. _____

10. _____

11. _____

12. _____

13. _____

14. _____

15. _____

16. _____

17. _____

18. _____

19. _____

20. _____

21. _____

22. _____

23. _____

24. _____

25. _____

Using Your Words:

Make as many words as you can from the letters in the following word.

falsehoods

_____

_____

_____

_____

_____

_____

_____

_____

_____

_____

Spelling Lesson:

As you hear them, write the spelling words for the day in the space provided. Be sure that you correct any words you have spelled incorrectly.

1. _____

2. _____

3. _____

4. _____

5. _____

6. _____

7. _____

8. _____

9. _____

10. _____

11. _____

12. _____

13. _____

14. _____

15. _____

16. _____

17. _____

18. _____

19. _____

20. _____

21. _____

22. _____

23. _____

24. _____

25. _____

Using Your Words:

Fill in the blanks with words from today's spelling list.

1. Last summer, I worked on an oil rig in the _____ .

2. When the firefighters arrived, the whole building was _____

   in flames.

3. After the movie, we _____our craving for ice cream.

4. Before winter came, Dad _____ all our windows and doors.

5. Paul Bunyan and his Blue Ox are part of Minnesota _____.

6. The _____ is a German _____ dance.

7. Jack took the _____of the sailboat so Dave could trim the sails.

8. My aunt was _____ at the outpouring of support for my

   uncle after his accident.

Day 144

As you hear them, write the spelling words for the day in the space provided. Be sure that you correct any words you have spelled incorrectly.

1. _____

2. _____

3. _____

4. _____

5. _____

6. _____

7. _____

8. _____

9. _____

10. _____

11. _____

12. _____

13. _____

14. _____

15. _____

16. _____

17. _____

18. _____

19. _____

20. _____

21. _____

22. _____

23. _____

24. _____

25. _____

Using Your Words:

Choose at least seven words from your spelling list and use them in a rhyme, poem, paragraph or silly story.

Spelling Lesson:

As you hear them, write the spelling words for the day in the space provided. Be sure that you correct any words you have spelled incorrectly.

1. _____

2. _____

3. _____

4. _____

5. _____

6. _____

7. _____

8. _____

9. _____

10. _____

11. _____

12. _____

13. _____

14. _____

15. _____

16. _____

17. _____

18. _____

19. _____

20. _____

21. _____

22. _____

23. _____

24. _____

25. _____

Using Your Words:

Fill in the blanks with words from today's spelling list.

1. One of the first things I learned in first aid was how to take my

   _____.

2. Last night, I had a sudden _____ to go for a bike ride.

3. Do you like sweet or _____ snacks better? I like the

   _____ in pretzels.

4. Steve and Jon played sentries in the school play. They had one line, "_____!

   Who goes there?"

5. The traffic tie up wasn't our _____, but it still made us late for the train.

6. The jury convicted him of _____ on a policeman and sentenced

   him to three months in jail.

7. Have you ever visited _____, Michigan?

8. Let's hope that the snow _____ won't cause too much

   flooding this spring.

Day 146

Spelling Lesson:

As you hear them, write the spelling words for the day in the space provided. Be sure that you correct any words you have spelled incorrectly.

1. _____

2. _____

3. _____

4. _____

5. _____

6. _____

7. _____

8. _____

9. _____

10. _____

11. _____

12. _____

13. _____

14. _____

15. _____

16. _____

17. _____

18. _____

19. _____

20. _____

21. _____

22. _____

23. _____

24. _____

25. _____

Using Your Words:

Make as many words as you can from the letters in the following word:

somersault

_____

_____

_____

_____

_____

_____

_____

_____

_____

Spelling Lesson:

As you hear them, write the spelling words for the day in the space provided. Be sure that you correct any words you have spelled incorrectly.

1. _____

2. _____

3. _____

4. _____

5. _____

6. _____

7. _____

8. _____

9. _____

10. _____

11. _____

12. _____

13. _____

14. _____

15. _____

16. _____

17. _____

18. _____

19. _____

20. _____

21. _____

22. _____

23. _____

24. _____

25. _____

Using Your Words:

Unscramble these:

1. corih _____

2. pielumvis _____

3. sneuvdloc _____

4. ddefaeult _____

5. srdoaeseultm _____

6. treselsw _____

7. eteldp _____

8. terlhse _____

9. dxleeat _____

10. mdeelt _____

Day 148

Spelling Lesson:

As you hear them, write the spelling words for the day in the space provided. Be sure that you correct any words you have spelled incorrectly.

1. _____

2. _____

3. _____

4. _____

5. _____

6. _____

7. _____

8. _____

9. _____

10. _____

11. _____

12. _____

13. _____

14. _____

15. _____

16. _____

17. _____

18. _____

19. _____

20. _____

21. _____

22. _____

23. _____

24. _____

25. _____

Using Your Words:

Choose at least seven words from your spelling list and use them in a short paragraph, silly story or poem.

Day 149

Spelling Lesson:

As you hear them, write the spelling words for the day in the space provided. Be sure that you correct any words you have spelled incorrectly.

1. _____

2. _____

3. _____

4. _____

5. _____

6. _____

7. _____

8. _____

9. _____

10. _____

11. _____

12. _____

13. _____

14. _____

15. _____

16. _____

17. _____

18. _____

19. _____

20. _____

21. _____

22. _____

23. _____

24. _____

25. _____

Using Your Words:

Fill in the blanks with words from today's spelling list.

1. Sarah's announcement came like a _____ out of the blue.

2. A bird will _____ at least once a year.

3. Allison will need to wait until next week for the _____ of her blood test.

4. Sometimes, it's _____ to overlook an _____ like that.

5. I hope that we can _____ this problem ourselves without involving an _____.

6. We need to stop at the drugstore and get some _____ for your sunburn.

Spelling Lesson:

As you hear them, write the spelling words for the day in the space provided. Be sure that you correct any words you have spelled incorrectly.

1. _____

2. _____

3. _____

4. _____

5. _____

6. _____

7. _____

8. _____

9. _____

10. _____

11. _____

12. _____

13. _____

14. _____

15. _____

16. _____

17. _____

18. _____

19. _____

20. _____

21. _____

22. _____

23. _____

24. _____

25. _____

Using Your Words:

List as many words as possible with the following letters (in order) in them.

olt
ult

Day 151

Spelling Lesson:

As you hear them, write the spelling words for the day in the space provided. Be sure that you correct any words you have spelled incorrectly.

1. _____

2. _____

3. _____

4. _____

5. _____

6. _____

7. _____

8. _____

9. _____

10. _____

11. _____

12. _____

13. _____

14. _____

15. _____

16. _____

17. _____

18. _____

19. _____

20. _____

21. _____

22. _____

23. _____

24. _____

25. _____

Using Your Words:

Unscramble these:

1. iitlfceusfdi   _____

2. dewalzt   _____

3. elvacs   _____

4. ueotdcnls   _____

5. itrlovenou   _____

6. emdtol   _____

7. sluteedr   _____

8. aaletcdutp   _____

9. ccotul   _____

10. basevlod   _____

Spelling Lesson:

As you hear them, write the spelling words for the day in the space provided. Be sure that you correct any words you have spelled incorrectly.

1. _____

2. _____

3. _____

4. _____

5. _____

6. _____

7. _____

8. _____

9. _____

10. _____

11. _____

12. _____

13. _____

14. _____

15. _____

16. _____

17. _____

18. _____

19. _____

20. _____

21. _____

22. _____

23. _____

24. _____

25. _____

Using Your Words

```
W  H  A  U  K  V  C  H  V  D  T  Z  R  N  S
B  M  G  U  V  V  W  D  V  E  A  E  S  O  O
G  Y  N  N  V  K  B  T  W  U  V  V  E  I  L
A  N  Z  F  I  F  R  A  Y  O  Y  Q  V  T  U
P  G  G  V  L  T  L  E  L  X  G  Y  L  U  T
N  O  I  T  A  T  L  U  S  N  O  C  A  L  I
D  L  E  P  Z  S  T  U  I  U  E  A  H  O  O
U  V  I  I  R  I  B  T  P  F  L  F  Q  S  N
A  C  N  I  O  K  L  Q  G  A  I  T  I  B  R
F  G  O  N  Y  U  Z  Q  W  N  T  I  I  A  P
K  H  A  C  S  S  X  Q  F  D  I  A  N  N  G
C  R  G  N  I  T  L  O  M  B  L  T  C  C  G
Y  E  I  S  P  A  G  H  E  T  T  I  L  R  A
Q  D  C  W  B  H  S  C  B  J  S  Q  B  O  S
S  X  U  D  S  D  Q  I  J  S  N  F  L  T  J
```

Words Used

absolution

catapulting

choirs

consultation

halves

insulting

jolting

molting

resulting

revolutionary

solution

spaghetti

waltzing

As you hear them, write the spelling words for the day in the space provided. Be sure that you correct any words you have spelled incorrectly.

1. _____

2. _____

3. _____

4. _____

5. _____

6. _____

7. _____

8. _____

9. _____

10. _____

11. _____

12. _____

13. _____

14. _____

15. _____

16. _____

17. _____

18. _____

19. _____

20. _____

21. _____

22. _____

23. _____

24. _____

25. _____

Using Your Words:

List as many words as possible with the following letters (in order) in them.

oblem

aim

_____

_____

_____

_____

_____

_____

_____

_____

_____

Day 154

Spelling Lesson:

As you hear them, write the spelling words for the day in the space provided. Be sure that you correct any words you have spelled incorrectly.

1. _____

2. _____

3. _____

4. _____

5. _____

6. _____

7. _____

8. _____

9. _____

10. _____

11. _____

12. _____

13. _____

14. _____

15. _____

16. _____

17. _____

18. _____

19. _____

20. _____

21. _____

22. _____

23. _____

24. _____

25. _____

Using Your Words:

Contraction practice
List the contraction that is formed by the two words

1. They are

2. There is _____

3. There are _____

4. It is _____

5. Is not _____

6. You are _____

7. We are _____

8. Were not _____

Day 155
Spelling Lesson:

As you hear them, write the spelling words for the day in the space provided. Be sure that you correct any words you have spelled incorrectly.

1. _____

2. _____

3. _____

4. _____

5. _____

6. _____

7. _____

8. _____

9. _____

10. _____

11. _____

12. _____

13. _____

14. _____

15. _____

16. _____

17. _____

18. _____

19. _____

20. _____

21. _____

22. _____

23. _____

24. _____

25. _____

Using Your Words:

Make as many words as you can from the following word:

pilgrimage

_____

_____

_____

_____

_____

_____

_____

_____

_____

_____

Day 156

As you hear them, write the spelling words for the day in the space provided. Be sure that you correct any words you have spelled incorrectly.

1. _____

2. _____

3. _____

4. _____

5. _____

6. _____

7. _____

8. _____

9. _____

10. _____

11. _____

12. _____

13. _____

14. _____

15. _____

16. _____

17. _____

18. _____

19. _____

20. _____

21. _____

22. _____

23. _____

24. _____

25. _____

Using Your Words:

Can you find the words?

```
I   W   E   B   A   T   H   O   G   E   S   G   C   N   E
T   S   I   D   X   K   Y   X   N   T   Y   N   O   Q   X
E   R   C   G   T   Z   J   C   G   J   S   I   N   U   C
M   E   M   I   W   A   S   N   Z   D   T   M   O   Z   L
I   M   B   N   U   A   I   I   F   A   E   M   I   R   A
Z   I   Z   C   A   M   M   G   M   M   M   A   T   C   M
A   A   S   E   I   Y   M   A   W   H   A   R   A   B   A
T   L   A   A   R   Q   L   A   I   K   T   G   M   X   T
I   C   M   D   O   C   G   B   R   Y   I   O   A   I   I
O   S   M   B   E   J   V   X   D   C   C   R   L   S   O
N   I   C   R   B   A   L   S   A   M   A   P   C   B   N
Y   D   L   A   C   I   T   A   M   E   L   B   O   R   P
K   M   Z   P   T   Z   E   C   H   L   L   O   R   T   Y
X   I   G   M   K   R   X   U   X   C   Y   G   P   C   K
U   W   I   A   C   C   L   A   M   A   T   I   O   N   O
```

Words used

acclamation

balsam

disclaimers

exclamation

itemization

maiming

problematical

proclamation

programming

reclamation

systematically

wigwam

321

Spelling Lesson:

As you hear them, write the spelling words for the day in the space provided. Be sure that you correct any words you have spelled incorrectly.

1. _____

2. _____

3. _____

4. _____

5. _____

6. _____

7. _____

8. _____

9. _____

10. _____

11. _____

12. _____

13. _____

14. _____

15. _____

16. _____

17. _____

18. _____

19. _____

20. _____

21. _____

22. _____

23. _____

24. _____

25. _____

Using Your Words:

whom/who

Whom can be either the object of the preposition or an object that receives the action of the verb. Examples: To **whom** are you speaking? Krista, in **whom** I have a lot of faith, wants to be the first female President.

Who is a subject that performs the action of the verb. Examples: **Who** goes to Harding High School? Larry, **who** loves nature, volunteers at the Parks Department.

Choose the correct pronoun in the sentences below:

1. I have a strong dislike for people (who, whom) lie to me.

2. Many of you have a friend with (who, whom) you entrust your deepest secrets.

3. Just looking at an airplane scares someone (who, whom) is afraid of flying.

4. (Who, Whom) did you say was calling?

5. The thief, (who, whom) stole the bicycle, was caught.

6. To (who, whom) should I give this letter?

7. I know the actor (who, whom) has the lead in that movie.

8. My grandmother, (who, whom) I loved very much, died last summer.

Day 158

Spelling Lesson:

As you hear them, write the spelling words for the day in the space provided. Be sure that you correct any words you have spelled incorrectly.

1. _____

2. _____

3. _____

4. _____

5. _____

6. _____

7. _____

8. _____

9. _____

10. _____

11. _____

12. _____

13. _____

14. _____

15. _____

16. _____

17. _____

18. _____

19. _____

20. _____

21. _____

22. _____

23. _____

24. _____

25. _____

Using Your Words:

Make as many words as you can from the letters in the following word:

thermometer

_____

_____

_____

_____

_____

_____

_____

_____

_____

Spelling Lesson:

As you hear them, write the spelling words for the day in the space provided. Be sure that you correct any words you have spelled incorrectly.

1. _____

2. _____

3. _____

4. _____

5. _____

6. _____

7. _____

8. _____

9. _____

10. _____

11. _____

12. _____

13. _____

14. _____

15. _____

16. _____

17. _____

18. _____

19. _____

20. _____

21. _____

22. _____

23. _____

24. _____

25. _____

Using Your Words:

Unscramble these:

1. ntmiaae   _____

2. oraiyfmlnl   _____

3. tsrthrommeee   _____

4. maapsibtl   _____

5. ioxaitacm   _____

6. isdoim   _____

7. rmupemi   _____

8. ruianmu   _____

9. gmauiern   _____

10. emordasn   _____

Day 160

As you hear them, write the spelling words for the day in the space provided. Be sure that you correct any words you have spelled incorrectly.

1. _____

2. _____

3. _____

4. _____

5. _____

6. _____

7. _____

8. _____

9. _____

10. _____

11. _____

12. _____

13. _____

14. _____

15. _____

16. _____

17. _____

18. _____

19. _____

20. _____

21. _____

22. _____

23. _____

24. _____

25. _____

Using your words:

Choose at least seven words from your spelling list and use them in a short paragraph, silly story or poem.

Evaluation Test #4

Fill in the blanks with the missing letters.

1. I just love Southern hospit_____.

2. I wish you would stop being so irrit_____.

3. Your handwriting is absolutely illeg_____.

4. Your work is incred_____ good.

5. We all have different respons_____ .

6. There ought to be room in the program for flex_____ .

7. Just what is tr_____ you?

8. I wish you would stop n_____ me.

9. That movie was just absolutely overwh_____ .

10. I would love to hear a rapper sing a f_____ song.

11. Everyone should have a good strong p_____.

12. There's no excuse for s_____ another person.

13. What a rev_____ development this is.

14. Have you ever kept a New Year's res_____ ?

15. What's the pr_____ ?

16. All syst_____ are go.

17. The governor procl_____ today as NOW day.

18. That was an official procl_____ .

19. Do you know the sym_____ of pellagra?

20. They held the school play in the audit_____.

Day 161

Spelling Lesson:

As you hear them, write the spelling words for the day in the space provided. Be sure that you correct any words you have spelled incorrectly.

1. _____

2. _____

3. _____

4. _____

5. _____

6. _____

7. _____

8. _____

9. _____

10. _____

11. _____

12. _____

13. _____

14. _____

15. _____

16. _____

17. _____

18. _____

19. _____

20. _____

21. _____

22. _____

23. _____

24. _____

25. _____

Using Your Words:

List as many words as you can that have the following letters (in order) in them.

amble

_____

_____

_____

_____

_____

_____

_____

_____

_____

_____

Day 162

As you hear them, write the spelling words for the day in the space provided. Be sure that you correct any words you have spelled incorrectly.

1. _____

2. _____

3. _____

4. _____

5. _____

6. _____

7. _____

8. _____

9. _____

10. _____

11. _____

12. _____

13. _____

14. _____

15. _____

16. _____

17. _____

18. _____

19. _____

20. _____

21. _____

22. _____

23. _____

24. _____

25. _____

Using your words:

Fill in the blanks with words from today's spelling list.

1. We are going to visit the _____ the next time we're in the city.

2. Last winter, my parents went to_____ to attend a health care _____.

3. How much do you think Tim _____ of his accident?

4. This year, we are growing green beans, peas, _____, and tomatoes in our garden.

5. After we _____ the bunk bed, we had to_____ it.

6. Our lake house has exposed _____ in the living room.

7. _____ will like the new casino that they're building in the city.

8. _____ is an ingredient in perfume that prevents evaporation.

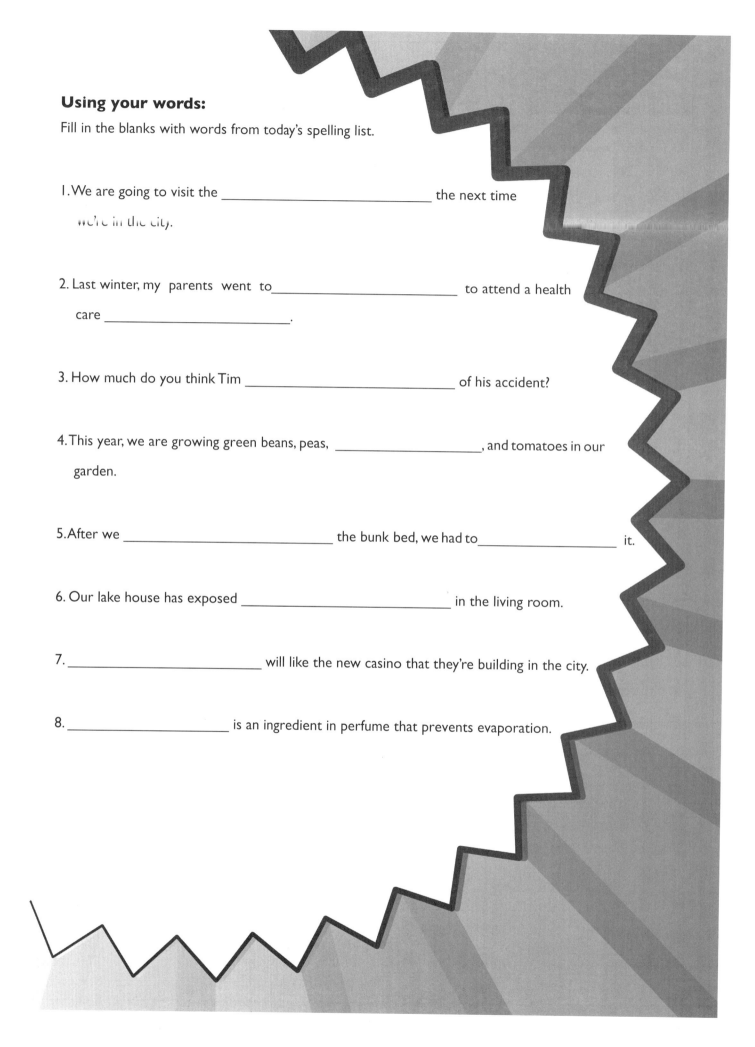

Day 163

As you hear them, write the spelling words for the day in the space provided. Be sure that you correct any words you have spelled incorrectly.

1. _____

2. _____

3. _____

4. _____

5. _____

6. _____

7. _____

8. _____

9. _____

10. _____

11. _____

12. _____

13. _____

14. _____

15. _____

16. _____

17. _____

18. _____

19. _____

20. _____

21. _____

22. _____

23. _____

24. _____

25. _____

Using Your Words:

Can you find the words?

```
M  A  M  R  E  Q  W  E  C  E  U  B  W  D  S
U  S  W  W  H  W  B  M  F  M  T  G  E  P  E
I  H  I  Q  P  H  X  S  B  R  K  L  J  S  P
R  E  M  E  M  B  E  R  E  D  B  Z  C  U  T
O  U  N  E  M  Q  S  Q  E  M  K  R  K  R  E
P  A  T  C  J  U  O  C  E  I  A  S  E  C  M
M  L  S  V  U  E  I  S  J  M  X  B  E  H  B
E  G  F  S  V  M  S  R  B  N  M  H  H  A  E
D  E  A  C  E  A  B  L  A  E  U  D  J  M  R
O  K  W  W  S  M  E  E  V  U  M  R  F  B  N
K  I  A  I  V  D  B  O  R  L  Q  J  M  E  A
O  I  D  A  N  Y  N  L  Y  E  L  A  V  R  R
M  U  I  R  A  L  O  S  Y  C  D  E  K  W  X
L  U  M  B  E  R  E  D  W  C  R  D  M  V  X
H  S  K  L  G  P  R  G  O  U  F  P  M  F  R
```

Words used

aquarium

assembly

chamber

disassembled

emporium

encumbered

lumbered

November

remembered

scrambled

September

solarium

Day 164
Spelling Lesson:

As you hear them, write the spelling words for the day in the space provided. Be sure that you correct any words you have spelled incorrectly.

1. _____

2. _____

3. _____

4. _____

5. _____

6. _____

7. _____

8. _____

9. _____

10. _____

11. _____

12. _____

13. _____

14. _____

15. _____

16. _____

17. _____

18. _____

19. _____

20. _____

21. _____

22. _____

23. _____

24. _____

25. _____

Using Your Words:

List as many words as you can that have the following letters (in order) in them.

disassembling

_____

_____

_____

_____

_____

_____

_____

_____

_____

_____

Spelling Lesson:

As you hear them, write the spelling words for the day in the space provided. Be sure that you correct any words you have spelled incorrectly.

1. _____

2. _____

3. _____

4. _____

5. _____

6. _____

7. _____

8. _____

9. _____

10. _____

11. _____

12. _____

13. _____

14. _____

15. _____

16. _____

17. _____

18. _____

19. _____

20. _____

21. _____

22. _____

23. _____

24. _____

25. _____

Using your words:

Fill in the blanks with words from today's spelling list.

1. My grandmother thinks I _____ my mom more

   than my dad.

2. Most of these clothes can be _____ dried.

3. When we were hiking, the large tree root caused me to _____

   and fall.

4. What's the _____ of the graduation party?

5. Appendicitis can sometimes cause _____ stomach pain.

6. Do you have a favorite _____? Mine is Chanel No. 5.

7. One of my little brother's chores is to _____ the trash each week.

8. After listening to the crowd _____ about the delay, the

   band decided to _____ playing.

Day 166

Spelling Lesson:

As you hear them, write the spelling words for the day in the space provided. Be sure that you correct any words you have spelled incorrectly.

1. _____   14. _____

2. _____   15. _____

3. _____   16. _____

4. _____   17. _____

5. _____   18. _____

6. _____   19. _____

7. _____   20. _____

8. _____   21. _____

9. _____   22. _____

10. _____   23. _____

11. _____   24. _____

12. _____   25. _____

13. _____

Using Your Words:

List as many words as you can that have the following letters (in order) in them.

umble
ume

_____

_____

_____

_____

_____

_____

_____

_____

_____

_____

Day 167

As you hear them, write the spelling words for the day in the space provided. Be sure that you correct any words you have spelled incorrectly.

1. _____

2. _____

3. _____

4. _____

5. _____

6. _____

7. _____

8. _____

9. _____

10. _____

11. _____

12. _____

13. _____

14. _____

15. _____

16. _____

17. _____

18. _____

19. _____

20. _____

21. _____

22. _____

23. _____

24. _____

25. _____

Using Your Words:

Unscramble these:

1   urpseem   _____

2   diebhum   _____

3   ustledmb   _____

4   legmirbsne   _____

5   iosmpatnsu   _____

6   txetrymie   _____

7   rdsemuep   _____

8   npsoimtnocu   _____

9   ohgtte   _____

10 ptemeid   _____

Day 168

As you hear them, write the spelling words for the day in the space provided. Be sure that you correct any words you have spelled incorrectly.

1. _____

2. _____

3. _____

4. _____

5. _____

6. _____

7. _____

8. _____

9. _____

10. _____

11. _____

12. _____

13. _____

14. _____

15. _____

16. _____

17. _____

18. _____

19. _____

20. _____

21. _____

22. _____

23. _____

24. _____

25. _____

Using your words:

Can you **find** the words?

E N L F C O S T U M I N G G L
O C B M J M J S Y R Z O N N D
Z F N G L V Z L V T E I B I B
P E T A M G E N Z B L T U M Q
S X Q V L M Y Z G B S P N U S
W P Y C E B Q J M B E M S S J
R X A R Q E M U U X O U T S A
T U P G X G R E H X I S U A R
X U L N H B N U S E Q E M A K
S P B Z Y E M I A E D R B A I
N R L E U B T T L W R P L G S
T X J G L U C T E B S C I L M
Y B R I R E F A I K M T N M L
O G N I Y T P M E I Y U G R K
I G L N I M B L Y W E N M V F

Words used

assuming

costuming

emptying

humbling

mumbling

nimbly

presumption

resemblance

rumbling

spaghetti

stumbling

supremely

Day 169

As you hear them, write the spelling words for the day in the space provided. Be sure that you correct any words you have spelled incorrectly.

1. _____

2. _____

3. _____

4. _____

5. _____

6. _____

7. _____

8. _____

9. _____

10. _____

11. _____

12. _____

13. _____

14. _____

15. _____

16. _____

17. _____

18. _____

19. _____

20. _____

21. _____

22. _____

23. _____

24. _____

25. _____

Using Your Words:

List as many words as you can that have the following letters (in order) in them.

temperature

_____

_____

_____

_____

_____

_____

_____

_____

_____

_____

Day 170

Spelling Lesson:

As you hear them, write the spelling words for the day in the space provided. Be sure that you correct any words you have spelled incorrectly.

1. _____

2. _____

3. _____

4. _____

5. _____

6. _____

7. _____

8. _____

9. _____

10. _____

11. _____

12. _____

13. _____

14. _____

15. _____

16. _____

17. _____

18. _____

19. _____

20. _____

21. _____

22. _____

23. _____

24. _____

25. _____

Using Your Words:

Unscramble these:

1. emrpspa _____

2. riheswmp _____

3. ormpser _____

4. smeisrp _____

5. alypm _____

6. smeapls _____

7. snouaitmn _____

8. rcaynltie _____

9. antufions _____

10. bgsaainr _____

Spelling Lesson:

As you hear them, write the spelling words for the day in the space provided. Be sure that you correct any words you have spelled incorrectly.

1. _____   14. _____

2. _____   15. _____

3. _____   16. _____

4. _____   17. _____

5. _____   18. _____

6. _____   19. _____

7. _____   20. _____

8. _____   21. _____

9. _____   22. _____

10. _____   23. _____

11. _____   24. _____

12. _____   25. _____

13. _____

Using Your Words:

Use each of the following spelling words in a sentence.

1. bumper _____

_____

2. mountainous _____

_____

3. villainous _____

_____

4. bargained _____

_____

5. simpered _____

_____

6. distemper _____

_____

7. pampered _____

_____

8. whimpered _____

_____

Sequential Spelling Level 4 - Student Workbook

Day 172

Spelling Lesson:

As you hear them, write the spelling words for the day in the space provided. Be sure that you correct any words you have spelled incorrectly.

1. _____

2. _____

3. _____

4. _____

5. _____

6. _____

7. _____

8. _____

9. _____

10. _____

11. _____

12. _____

13. _____

14. _____

15. _____

16. _____

17. _____

18. _____

19. _____

20. _____

21. _____

22. _____

23. _____

24. _____

25. _____

Using your words:

Choose at least ten words from your spelling list and use them in a short paragraph, silly story or poem.

Spelling Lesson:

As you hear them, write the spelling words for the day in the space provided. Be sure that you correct any words you have spelled incorrectly.

1. _____

2. _____

3. _____

4. _____

5. _____

6. _____

7. _____

8. _____

9. _____

10. _____

11. _____

12. _____

13. _____

14. _____

15. _____

16. _____

17. _____

18. _____

19. _____

20. _____

21. _____

22. _____

23. _____

24. _____

25. _____

Using Your Words:

List as many words as you can that have the following letters (in order) in them.

ain
ean
ian

_____

_____

_____

_____

_____

_____

_____

_____

Day 174

Spelling Lesson:

As you hear them, write the spelling words for the day in the space provided. Be sure that you correct any words you have spelled incorrectly.

1. _____

2. _____

3. _____

4. _____

5. _____

6. _____

7. _____

8. _____

9. _____

10. _____

11. _____

12. _____

13. _____

14. _____

15. _____

16. _____

17. _____

18. _____

19. _____

20. _____

21. _____

22. _____

23. _____

24. _____

25. _____

Using Your Words:

Fill in the blank using words from today's spelling list.

1. The _____ and the Democrats are the two major political parties in the United States.

2. We enjoy drinking _____ coffee.

3. Residents of Canada are called _____.

4. Since her family is from Norway, my mom sometimes wears a tradional _____ costume.

5. Genghis Khan was from _____.

6. When we went to the beach last summer, we saw lots of _____ near the pier.

7. I helped my mom sew new _____ for the kitchen.

8. My sister Katie met lots of _____ when she visited Australia last year.

Day 175

Spelling Lesson:

As you hear them, write the spelling words for the day in the space provided. Be sure that you correct any words you have spelled incorrectly.

1. _____

2. _____

3. _____

4. _____

5. _____

6. _____

7. _____

8. _____

9. _____

10. _____

11. _____

12. _____

13. _____

14. _____

15. _____

16. _____

17. _____

18. _____

19. _____

20. _____

21. _____

22. _____

23. _____

24. _____

25. _____

Using Your Words:

Unscramble these:

1. tanBrii   _____

2. atcedinpa   _____

3. franfiu   _____

4. ygooleth   _____

5. eirbtrnnua   _____

6. abairAn   _____

7. sCiraithn   _____

8. noogaMlin   _____

9. elegclo   _____

10. iandanl   _____

Spelling Lesson:

As you hear them, write the spelling words for the day in the space provided. Be sure that you correct any words you have spelled incorrectly.

1. _____

2. _____

3. _____

4. _____

5. _____

6. _____

7. _____

8. _____

9. _____

10. _____

11. _____

12. _____

13. _____

14. _____

15. _____

16. _____

17. _____

18. _____

19. _____

20. _____

21. _____

22. _____

23. _____

24. _____

25. _____

Using Your Words:

Make as many words
as you can from the
following word:

toboggans

_____

_____

_____

_____

_____

_____

_____

_____

_____

_____

Day 177

Spelling Lesson:

As you hear them, write the spelling words for the day in the space provided. Be sure that you correct any words you have spelled incorrectly.

1. _____

2. _____

3. _____

4. _____

5. _____

6. _____

7. _____

8. _____

9. _____

10. _____

11. _____

12. _____

13. _____

14. _____

15. _____

16. _____

17. _____

18. _____

19. _____

20. _____

21. _____

22. _____

23. _____

24. _____

25. _____

Using Your Words

Fill in the blanks with words from today's spelling list.

1. When did _____ lights come to your dad's farm?

2. Do you like classical _____? I do.

3. _____ is the largest of the seven continents.

4. The economy was the most important _____ in the campaign last fall.

5. Janet carefully unwrapped the _____ from her gift.

6. _____ is the Spanish word for beans.

7. Sometimes I think I need a _____ wand to get all my projects done.

8. Jack's favorite subject is _____ .

Spelling Lesson:

As you hear them, write the spelling words for the day in the space provided. Be sure that you correct any words you have spelled incorrectly.

1. _____

2. _____

3. _____

4. _____

5. _____

6. _____

7. _____

8. _____

9. _____

10. _____

11. _____

12. _____

13. _____

14. _____

15. _____

16. _____

17. _____

18. _____

19. _____

20. _____

21. _____

22. _____

23. _____

24. _____

25. _____

Using Your Words:

Unscramble these:

1. oiitpilanc   _____

2. cumaiisn   _____

3. osiirtneactb   _____

4. acnyishpi   _____

5. gicaainm   _____

6. cetilceianr   _____

7. sinarEua   _____

8. iPninaheoc   _____

9. rnPsiae   _____

10. iucCasana   _____

Day 179

Spelling Lesson:

As you hear them, write the spelling words for the day in the space provided. Be sure that you correct any words you have spelled incorrectly.

1. _____

2. _____

3. _____

4. _____

5. _____

6. _____

7. _____

8. _____

9. _____

10. _____

11. _____

12. _____

13. _____

14. _____

15. _____

16. _____

17. _____

18. _____

19. _____

20. _____

21. _____

22. _____

23. _____

24. _____

25. _____

Using Your Words:

Can you  the words?

```
O  M  X  P  D  L  Q  U  P  H  T  X  F  S  S
N  B  A  O  E  E  P  K  F  P  T  P  R  T  N
S  F  S  N  A  I  C  I  T  I  L  O  P  A  A
C  N  A  T  P  A  R  I  S  I  A  N  S  T  I
U  K  A  S  E  E  I  N  T  N  D  T  S  I  C
S  Z  W  I  H  T  A  I  U  B  E  W  Q  S  I
H  X  W  P  C  I  R  K  D  C  Q  S  R  T  G
I  M  Q  G  C  U  O  I  H  X  M  S  A  I  A
O  X  X  I  M  I  F  N  C  S  W  D  P  C  M
N  C  T  W  S  C  I  N  E  I  D  K  K  I  H
M  P  D  S  K  C  B  F  O  D  A  Y  F  A  I
O  O  U  U  I  E  F  U  N  C  B  N  K  N  X
M  E  E  A  C  X  O  I  Y  S  F  H  S  S  R
D  B  N  B  L  E  W  Q  Q  Y  R  F  K  O  M
A  S  F  M  R  V  H  H  K  K  J  V  X  U  V
```

Words used

Confucians

cushion

fashioned

issued

magicians

obstetricians

opticians

Parisians

politicians

statisticians

technicians

Day 180

Spelling Lesson:

As you hear them, write the spelling words for the day in the space provided. Be sure that you correct any words you have spelled incorrectly.

1. _____

2. _____

3. _____

4. _____

5. _____

6. _____

7. _____

8. _____

9. _____

10. _____

11. _____

12. _____

13. _____

14. _____

15. _____

16. _____

17. _____

18. _____

19. _____

20. _____

21. _____

22. _____

23. _____

24. _____

25. _____

Using your words:

Choose at least seven words from your spelling list and use them in a short paragraph, silly story or poem.

Final Evaluation Test

Fill in the blanks with the missing letters.

1. We have some unfin_____ business to attend to.

2. Actors just love appl_____.

3. Famil_____ breeds contempt.

4. My older sister is an electri_____.

5. A teacher spe_____ izes in helping people learn.

6. Do you like previews of comng attr_____?

7. How many of the psychic's pre_____ came true?

8. How do you think I arrived at that concl_____?

9. We gave them new sw_____ for their anniversary.

10. My sister works for a constr_____ company.

11. Do you like standing in a re_____ line?

12. Most people enjoy going to a wedding re_____.

13.   Cattle are sl_____ everyday in stockyards.

14.   Some people are very imp_____ .

15.   The mayor was unav_____ . for comment

16.   I just love Southern hospit_____ .

17.   We all have different respons_____ .

18.   Have you ever kept a New Year's resol_____ ?

19.   The governor procl _____ today as NOW day.

20.   That was an official procl_____ .

21.   Have you re_____ everything I've taught you?

22.   Never eat scr_____ eggs that have turned green.

23.   Be careful when making an ass_____ about anything.

24.   I hate to hear a dog wh_____ .

25.   I have a friend who has become a veget_____ .

NEW YORK

Story Starters

Sometimes, pictures can inspire us to write poems or stories. Take a look at the picture above. What do you think happened before and after? Has something similar happened to you? How did you react? Think about these questions as you write a short poem or story about this picture.

Story Starters

Sometimes, pictures can inspire us to write poems or stories. Take a look
at the picture above. What do you think happened before and after? Has
something similar happened to you? How did you react? Think about these
questions as you write a short poem or story about this picture.

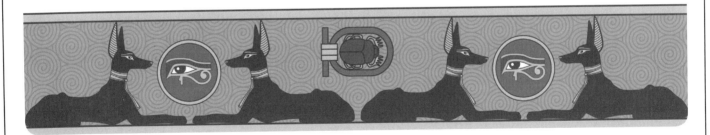

Story Starters

Sometimes, pictures can inspire us to write poems or stories. Take a look at the picture above. What do you think happened before and after? Has something similar happened to you? How did you react? Think about these questions as you write a short poem or story about this picture.

Story Starters

Sometimes, pictures can inspire us to write poems or stories. Take a look at the picture above. What do you think happened before and after? Has something similar happened to you? How did you react? Think about these questions as you write a short poem or story about this picture.